Routledge Performance Practitioners is a series of introductory guides to the key theater-makers of the last century. Each volume explains the background to and the work of one of the major influences on twentieth- and twenty-first-century performance.

Rudolf Laban was one of the leading dance theorists of the twentieth century. His work on dance analysis and notation raised the status of dance as both an art form and a scholarly discipline. This is the first book to combine:

- an overview of Laban's life, work and influences
- an exploration of his key ideas, including the revolutionary "Laban Movement Analysis" system
- analysis of his works *Die Grünen Clowns* and *The Mastery of Movement* and their relevance to dance theater from the 1920s onwards
- a detailed exercise-based breakdown of Laban's key teachings.

As a first step towards critical understanding, and as an initial exploration before going on to further primary research, **Routledge Performance Practitioners** are   oday's student.

Karen K. Bradley   r and Director of Graduate

Studies i   ʾark. She is a

Certified

ROUTLEDGE PERFORMANCE PRACTITIONERS

Series editor: Franc Chamberlain, University College Cork

Routledge Performance Practitioners is an innovative series of introductory handbooks on key figures in twentieth-century performance
practice. Each volume focuses on a theater-maker whose practical and
theoretical work has in some way transformed the way we understand
theater and performance. The books are carefully structured to enable
the reader to gain a good grasp of the fundamental elements underpinning each practitioner's work. They will provide an inspiring
springboard for future study, unpacking and explaining what can
initially seem daunting.

The main sections of each book cover:

- personal biography
- explanation of key writings
- description of significant productions
- reproduction of practical exercises.

Volumes currently available in the series are:

Eugenio Barba by Jane Turner
Pina Bausch by Royd Climenhaga
Augusto Boal by Frances Babbage
Bertolt Brecht by Meg Mumford
Michael Chekhov by Franc Chamberlain
Jacques Copeau by Mark Evans
Etienne Decroux by Thomas Leabhart
Jerzy Grotowski by James Slowiak and Jairo Cuesta
Anna Halprin by Libby Worth and Helen Poyner
Rudolf Laban by Karen K. Bradley
Robert Lepage by Aleksandar Dundjerovic
Ariane Mnouchkine by Judith G. Miller
Jacques Lecoq by Simon Murray
Joan Littlewood by Nadine Holdsworth
Vsevolod Meyerhold by Jonathan Pitches

Konstantin Stanislavsky by Bella Merlin

Hijikata Tatsumi and Ohno Kazuo by Sondra Horton Fraleigh and
    Tamah Nakamura

Mary Wigman by Mary Ann Santos Newhall

Robert Wilson by Maria Shevtsova

Future volumes will include:

Marina Abramović
Antonin Artaud
Peter Brook
Tadeusz Kantor
Richard Schechner
Lee Strasberg

RUDOLF LABAN

Karen K. Bradley

Routledge
Taylor & Francis Group

LONDON AND NEW YORK

First published 2009
by Routledge
2 Park Square, Milton Park, Abingdon, Oxon OX14 4RN

Simultaneously published in the USA and Canada
by Routledge
270 Madison Ave, New York, NY 10016

Routledge is an imprint of the Taylor & Francis Group, an informa business

Typeset in Perpetua by Taylor & Francis Books
Printed and bound in Great Britain by
TJ International Ltd, Padstow, Cornwall

British Library Cataloguing in Publication Data
A catalogue record for this book is available from the British Library

Library of Congress Cataloging in Publication Data
  Bradley, Karen K., 1951–
  Rudolph Laban / Karen K. Bradley. — 1st ed.
    p. cm. — (Routledge performance practitioners)
  Includes bibliographical references and index.
  1. Laban, Rudolf von, 1879–1958. 2. Choreographers—Hungary—
Biography. 3. Tanztheater—History. I. Title.
  GV1785.L2B73 2008
 792.8'2092—dc22

                                                    2008011129

ISBN10: 0-415-37524-X (hbk)
ISBN10: 0-415-37525-8 (pbk)
ISBN10: 0-203-09896-X (ebk)

ISBN13: 978-0-415-37524-5 (hbk)
ISBN13: 978-0-415-37525-2 (pbk)
ISBN13: 978-0-203-09896-7 (ebk)

CONTENTS

LIST OF FIGURES

PREFACE

The research for this short book has been comprehensive and far-ranging. I decided to approach my analysis and synthesis of Laban's life and work the same way we movement analysts approach applying his work to research: I observed the data about his life and work, heard stories, and read documents looking for the details and the nuances. I examined scribbled notes and spoke with people who knew him. I also stepped back and tried to see his life and work within the meta-frame of the twentieth century. This micro/macro pattern analysis is the very essence of Laban's thinking and of his concepts and practices.

The macro/micro analysis is only one of the many dichotomies addressed in the book, however. Teasing phenomena into polar opposites and defining continua along the polarities is at the heart of Laban's work, and at the core of his personality as well. Laban lived through times of increasing complexity, and his theories reflect a categorical approach to movement analysis as well as a synthesis of opposites into a whole. The resulting system can appear overly specific or loosely general. In effect, Laban's work is organic in origin, arising from experimentation and play, and systematic in application, particularly as standardization of vocabulary and symbols were required for archival purposes.

Writing about Laban's theory of movement, including his vocabulary for discerning the full range of nonverbal communication possibilities is a challenge. People who study the work and receive advanced level certification in it know that it takes much practice, reflection, insight and dialogue to arrive at an embodied understanding rather than mere intellectual knowledge of the movement analysis.

As a result, my conclusions about the nature and intent of Laban's work are in some cases different from those of some previous biographers. My approach was both as an insider/initiate—someone who has studied Laban's work in depth and experientially for years—and as a curious researcher. I tried to stay open to the essence and nature of a man I never met or observed directly, while interpreting what I was hearing, reading or seeing on film through the lens of the Laban Movement Analysis work itself, work I have been actively engaged in practicing and shaping for over twenty years.

I also hoped to let Mr Laban speak for himself, to find quotes from his published and unpublished writings that reflected the underlying values and principles inherent in the work. I was fortunate to open boxes and discover resonant bits of writing, drawings, charts and graphs that revealed yet another corner of the room that was his body-mind. I was equally fortunate to find able translators in the European Certified Movement Analyst (CMA) community who could not only translate the words, but also help me to contextualize the thinking.

As a dance educator and historian, as well as a choreographer and coach, to me, Laban's approach to creating and performing dance and dance-theater has been influential to how much work is created in the theater, on films, online and in the site-specific locations of twenty-first century creative work. I hope that this book contributes to an increasing recognition of his place within the continuum of performance art.

Over twenty-five years ago, I began studying the Laban work because, of all the approaches I find effective for building the performer's repertoire, the Laban work is the one that continues to provide more pathways, more branches off, more applications and new journeys. I have never seen the end of the road. The work continues to grow in me and to inform my understanding and interactions with the world as a choreographer, writer, teacher, coach and activist.

ACKNOWLEDGMENTS

I am indebted to many people for this little book, which is the result of much analysis of archival data. First of all, thanks to Sondra Fraleigh for suggesting me. Viv Bridson led me to her and John Hodgson's collection of Laban's materials that he (Laban) had left in Germany when he fled to France. This collection, now at the University of Leeds, contained so many delightful surprises that other scholars will be able to have a field day and learn much more than I was able to write about here. Viv is a repository of details about Laban's life, and I am personally and eternally grateful.

I could not have begun to take the information found in Valerie Preston-Dunlop's comprehensive biography, *Rudolf Laban: An Extraordinary Life*, to such a level, had Valerie herself not provided additional access to her own interpretations and understanding. I am thankful to her for her book, and also for the extra insights she has personally provided.

Antja Kennedy housed me; spent hours with me on her own knowledge of Laban's work and enriched this book considerably. She also introduced me to Annette Heesen and Sabine Fichter, who translated materials in the Köln and Leipzig tanz-archivs respectively, and who took such wonderful care of me while I was there.

The dance archivists/librarians at the collections include: Helen Roberts at the University of Surrey; the staff at Laban; Thomas

Thorausch at the Köln Archives; and Dr Janine Schulze Geschefts, Business Director, and Gabriele Ruiz, Librarian, in Leipzig. By lucky chance, Evelyn Dörr was doing her own research at the Leipzig archives the day I was there, and she has been so generous with her time and historical knowledge; much of my unpacking of *The Green Clowns* comes from her.

I am also grateful to Yvonne Widger and the professionals at the Dartington Hall Trust Archives, where I found the translation Mr Laban made of the speech he gave in 1936 in front of Dr Paul Joseph Goebbels, Minister of Culture.

I have had much support from my colleagues at the University of Maryland, especially Charles Rutherford, my Chair for much of this project, Alcine Wiltz and Anne Warren, fellow CMAs and supportive colleagues, and Phyllis Crowther and Marie Visosky, who make the trains run on time, and ensure that I am on them.

The photographs are of my colleagues Alcine Wiltz, Anne Warren and Gretchen Dunn, along with students Megan Merchant, Ling Tang and Nilay Arioz, beautiful movers all. The photographs themselves are the product of Thai Nguyen, photographer at the University of Maryland.

Thanks also to my colleagues at the Laban/Bartenieff Institute of Movement Studies in New York City and in Maryland, each of whom has nurtured both me and parts of the book: Jackie Hand, Karen Studd, Laura Cox, Lynn Wenning Adelmann, Esther Geiger, Jaye Knutson, Tomi Casciero, Eileen Jones, Jody Arnhold, Virginia Reed, Bob Bejan, Jan Whitener, Luis Cancel, Keith Sedlacek, Jane Bonbright, Bala Sarasvati, Ellen Goldman, Linda Nutter, Eleanor Weisman, Martha Eddy, Janet Hamburg, and so many others have enriched my own understanding of the work we do. Janet Kaylo and I began interviewing some of the "Laban Ladies" together many years ago, and video shot by Patrick Lears has been very useful. Megan Reisel and I also shared video and interviews, and the footage and quotes she has were inspiring. Warren Lamb has always been generous with his insights, Sam Thornton delightful, and the stories that Betty Meredith-Jones, Geraldine Stephenson, Walli Meier, Marion North, Susi Thornton and Jean Newlove shared augmented those of Viv Bridson and Valerie Preston-Dunlop in personal and colorful ways!

Gretchen Dunn has been an incredible supporter of this book; she continues to be a gift to the Laban community in many ways. Malcolm Shute helped immensely with feedback and editing suggestions. Naima

Prevots gave much feedback and support. I am also grateful to Jan Whitener for her belief in this work and her commitment to seeing it help others. And to Regina Miranda, Executive Director of LIMS and so very much more, I can only bow deeply and say "BIG KISS!"

To my children, Cleo, Dana and Larry: thank you for forbearance and lost weekends. Bethany, you are always with me.

My editor, Franc Chamberlain, has been patient and encouraging. I look forward to any future endeavors.

And finally, to my husband, Richard Bell; he of the red pen and evil smile: this book is yours; without your editorial slash-and-burn approach, the book would be quite full of indefinite antecedents and jargon. You have been the best support of all, whether you wield the pen or the cooking spoon. Mr Laban, all CMAs, and I owe you.

LABAN'S CORE

Biography

Rudolf Laban never planned anything in his life. As a true visionary, life for him was one long improvisation. He described himself as a salamander, and it is possible to see him that way—eyes darting to see everything, quick, constantly advancing. He has also been described as a genius, a manipulator and a womanizer—all of which turn out to be facets of this complex man; a man without a plan, but a man with a purpose. His purpose was to move ahead and to spread out. In photographs, he is leaning forward peering at us, challenging us to respond, to grab hold of the essence of life. His eyes have a twinkle in them. The twinkle is mischievous.

He never owned his own intellectual property; ideas flowed through him, coming from a vast number of sources, passing through his continually active mind and body, where he readily disbursed them to his followers. He did not see his work as a commodity. Despite the fact that money was always a problem for him, his work was not for sale.

Mary Wigman described him as a "great wanderer." (Wigman and Sorell, 1973, p. 32) Vera Maletic added that wherever he stayed, even if for a short while, he left his traces. (1987, p. 13)

Mary Wigman (1886–1973) was a choreographer and student of Laban's. She is considered one of the founders of modern dance in Germany.

To him, it was simple. In Laban's world, life was movement and movement was life. He was master of both the instant and the long-range horizon. Laban was also a recycler; he was pragmatic, opportunistic and conservative in the sense of making the best of a situation and the materials at hand, in the moment. At the same time, he saw the range of possibilities across a broad spectrum. Laban's view of the horizon did not lead to his forming intentions, however. The horizon merely provided a canvas for possibilities.

Some portray him as a trickster, and he loved play and playfulness. He was definitely a provocateur as well. But even though he could be quite naïve, he was no fool. He was a keen observer and saw human impulses and predilections that needed to come to fruition. He watched, and listened, and responded as a man fully in touch with the realities around him. Only in his political astuteness did he fail to attend soon enough; he admired power and so, as we shall see, became entangled with the Nazis for a time.

Laban was both naive and wise. He was open to new possibilities and viewpoints and he could be dogmatic at times as well. Laban looked at phenomena from many perspectives. Some say he could see the trace forms of movement and the energies behind gestures. The desire to tap into and amplify the human movement story is what drew him to the theater. (Kennedy Interview, July 8, 2004)

His student and colleague Kurt Jooss said that Laban's main interest was always a kind of educative and therapeutic approach. "He believed in the salvation of the science of dancing" (Partsch-Bergsohn and Jooss, 2002). In 1920, Laban even told Jooss that dancing would develop and would rescue a dissolute society.

Kurt Jooss (1901–1979) was a dancer with Laban's Tanzbühne in the late 1910s and 1920s. He eventually established his own company, combining ballet with the tanztheater work, and is best known for his antiwar ballet, *The Green Table* (1932).

Laban's life story is a tale of aspiration to deliverance and transcendence, but it is not the story of how he saved society. It is a story about the gifts of salvation and transcendence that he tried to give humanity, through movement. As we look at the last 150 or more years since Laban's birth, it is clear that humanity has, thus far, tended to ignore the gift.

DEVELOPING

Laban was born December 15, 1879, in Bratislava, the oldest of three children and the only boy. His father was an officer in the Austro-Hungarian army and his mother often traveled with her husband, leaving young Rudolf alone with his grandparents. From the hills above Bratislava, then called Poszny or Pressburg, he gained perspective. Looking down on the town: the church spires, the twisting streets and shops, the theater, and most vividly, the series of town squares, he could see humans in interaction, in expression, in community and in commerce. He could also see the heavens; majestic, and massive, and sense his own small place within them. It was there in those hills that he first came upon the interweaving of nature and metropolis, the individual and the community, the quotidian and the performative that informed his later work.

His early teenage years were full of travel: to Sarajevo, Mostar, Istanbul and the like. Since his father was an officer, such deployments were not uncommon. As an inventive and self-possessed child, Laban roamed the countryside in these locales on his own. The natural formations of rocks, trees and terrain created a backdrop and set for his imaginative stories and plays. Local myths and folklore culture played an influential role in his creations of plays and puppet shows, and because of the travels, he picked up an international banquet of tales.

During his travels, Laban was exposed to both eastern and western sensibilities, studying under an Imam for a time.

> He drank in Middle Eastern philosophy and sacred practices ... Russian Orthodox Catholicism, Greek Orthodoxy, Turkish-style Muslim concepts and behaviour, extremist Sufi practices, as well as Catholic and Protestant Christian groups, all contributed to his awareness of religious possibilities and human behaviour.
>
> (Preston-Dunlop, 1998, p. 3)

While in Istanbul, according to Valarie Preston-Dunlop, he also encountered Sufism and Dervish dances. The exposure to mysticism, the crossing of boundaries between the waking and dreaming world, provided

Laban with a holistic sensibility, launching him on a lifelong search for hidden meanings and allegorical symbology.

He was attracted to performance—theatrical, military, story-telling, puppetry; all forms of nonverbal, movement-based forms of human discourse. He wrote about his childhood Kasperl Theater (a Punch and Judy type of puppet stage). The character of Kasperl was based on his actor-uncle, Adolf Mylius, (who had become a sort of black sheep of the family); and the devil character was called Napoleum, after Napoleon; these players conspired to find a blue flower that renders the finder immortal. The devil was banished and there was a joyful dance at the end. Laban, in *A Life for Dance* (written on the eve of the rise of Nazi Germany), concludes: "My childhood play has a happy ending. Time has taught me to think differently. It is the devil who more often than not gets to keep the blue flower" (1975, p. 9).

His relationship with his father was convoluted. As a military man, Papa Laban was not pleased that his only son chose the life of an artist over following in his footsteps. Nevertheless, Laban's father supported him financially through his turbulent years as a young artist in Paris.

His mother was more of a playmate. A painter, and a woman with liberal, if not socialist leanings, Marie von Laban encouraged the imaginative play and spectacles in which her son engaged.

During his later teenage years, the family lived in Budapest, where Rudolf was a bit of a man-about-town. Photos from this time show a dark-haired, slender, intensely focused man-boy, with an expressive eyebrow, and a sophisticated air. The family was upper-middle class and Laban was the oldest and a male. The city of Budapest had become a cosmopolitan and sophisticated Mecca for the Empire and the coffeehouses rivaled those of Vienna. In many ways, Laban could have easily wound up a shallow cad, for the café-society called him and he responded with enthusiasm.

But the muses also came calling early on and he was pulled in artistic directions and subsequently adopted a more focused and disciplined attitude than he might otherwise have had. Despite a privileged, but often lonely childhood, he had learned to observe human behavior. This visual perceptivity led him in the direction of the visual arts.

Laban was first drawn to painting as a vocation, primarily due to the tutelage of an artist whose values of "love of work, scrupulous fulfillment of duty and unaffected behaviour" (1975, p. 10) were a contrast with the indulged life he had been living as the only son of a high-ranking officer. As his visual training evolved, however, he began to see the movement within the static picture:

> It needed a special occasion to open my eyes to the fact that in the "moving picture" lies hidden a tremendously enhanced expression of human will and feeling ... Then came a memorable day when I discovered tableaux vivants.
>
> (Laban, 1975, p. 11)

He put together a series of these tableaux, with musical accompaniment, in such a way that each moment built on the last. When strung together, the theatricality and evolution of the static scenes took on movement and drama. He was still in his teen years when he built such tableaux; he was also apprenticed to a scenic painter for a time.

By the late 1890s, along with many writers and thinkers in Budapest, he was caught between the old world of traditions and stories, which he understood as powerful and compelling, and the emerging questioning of the direction of human culture. This struggle was far more than a man versus machine concern. The reconciliation of old and new was being played out across the western world. Laban's particular and personal struggles led directly to the evolution of his theories and practice.

TRAINING AND STUDYING

Laban entered into officer training for the Austrian–Hungarian army in 1899, into the Military Academy at Wiener Neustadt, near Vienna, at the behest, if not direct order of his father.

His training included riding, social dancing, military maneuvers, fencing, French, German, and "nationalist dogma" (Preston-Dunlop, 1998, p. 6). Within a year and a half, Laban quit, through with the conformist training. He had always been an erratic student—bright but difficult—and the Army of the Emperor found him engaged in the same struggle.

Even as a child, he had been taken with the patterns of military parades, and fencing and social dance patterns also interested him. His intense training in these latter two areas, particularly, informed his personal movement skills. But the parades, large colorful sweeping patterns in which the individual skills of the performers were subsumed, may have been an inspiration for his improvisational choirs later on.

He struggled with both a fascination for the machine, particularly the reliability and discipline that repetitive functional movement and spectacle provided, and for the artistic soul of the individual. He appreciated the particulars of folk dance and the agrarian lifestyle as well as the attractions of high culture and urban life. The academy at Wiener Neustadt afforded him access to all manner of society, but in the end, the desire to live the life of an artist won out.

His father was not pleased with his choice to leave the training academy, but provided support and letters of introduction, as well as financial support for Laban and his new bride, Martha Fricke, to set up household in Munich. It is not clear how Laban and Martha met, but both had aspirations as visual artists and Fricke was already a painter.

EXPLORING MUNICH AND PARIS

Munich in 1898–99 was an up-and-coming center for what would become expressionist art. Art Nouveau was in the ascendancy at the time Laban and Martha arrived, and it was in Munich that he was influenced by Hermann Obrist, a sculptor. Obrist was interested in the modern and the abstract but, more significantly, he worked in many different media forms.

Hermann Obrist (1863–1927) was a German sculptor and part of the Art Nouveau movement. Art Nouveau was popular from about 1880–1914 (World War I) and was a form of design that consisted of curving, flowing, elegant lines, incorporating plants and flowers.

Munich's artists were shifting from romanticism to expressionism. Laban was influenced by all schools and ultimately found himself creating in the spaces between story and abstraction, physicality and expression. He was a man influenced by many sources and he lived in a time when the arts, sciences, psychology and social theories were all converging. Laban began to think about his own path, which had, up to this point been largely unclear. His barely articulated quest was to find a form of performance that allowed the individual to speak with his/her own voice, to contribute to a greater whole, and that allowed group access to the larger concerns of the human condition.

According to Valerie Preston-Dunlop (Interview, July 3, 2004), Laban started in Munich as a pageant director. He was hired to create a comic carnival piece based in a profession. Given a brief and asked to do it, he came up with the idea of an improvised group dance. Later on, the group work would become far more formalized but even in these early days, he valued both individual and group input.

Laban was deeply concerned with questions about the nature of the individual versus the group. He was developing his philosophy and life choices at the same time that many were reading Marx and Engels, Freud, and anarchists like Michael Bakunin. The very nature of government, of democracy, of capitalism, of culture was being questioned by writers, activists and artists. And the role of the individual within the concerns of the group became a seminal issue of the twentieth century.

Laban loved the mystical, the grotesque and the circus. He knew the sources of play and storytelling as well as the underlying layers of tragedy within those forms. He unpacked the layers readily, and observed as the stories and images that were revealed took form as visual and plastic art.

After he and Martha moved to Paris in 1900, he tried to enroll in various studios and ecoles. It is clear from his subsequent drawings and architectural designs that he did study, but according to Preston-Dunlop (1998, p. 10), his name did not appear on any of the rolls at that time. Martha's did, however. She was enrolled at the Ecole des Beaux Arts School of Architecture in 1903.

Laban and Martha both participated in the café life and the salons. There, the blend of spiritualism and decadence that prevailed led to his early commentaries and works based on this period. The early days in the Paris café scene laid the groundwork for his depth of understanding of the light and dark forces that an artist draws on for creative work. In *A Life for Dance*, he described his attempts, some years later, to capture the dichotomies of the café society that both fascinated and repelled him:

> Has art, so passionately defended as the great provider of happiness and peace, any place amidst this hustle? How can true beauty dwell among the glitter of tattered silk and under the artificial purple lights? How can the soul

> rejoice amid the rags of the poor and the hollow eyes of hungry children? How
> utterly remote is the fragrance of the mountains and forests from the air of the
> slums, so thick with coal-dust and from the deadly smell of the powdered
> prostitute! Is that the song of man? I wondered in horror.
>
> (Laban, 1975, p. 43)

This somewhat Victorian and judgmental perspective on what was attractive to him as well as repellant did not spring from either an overdose of religiosity or any type of atheism. Laban was highly spiritual but he did not ascribe to any one spiritual practice; he was not a cultist. He was attracted to practices that expanded perception rather than allowing himself to fall under the spell of unexamined beliefs. He was willing to experience the beliefs of any aspect of society and to apply this perspective to his creative work. In the end, his openness was part of his aesthetic, one of his many talents, and later informed the development of his theories.

Laban's journey almost ended, however, when Martha died in 1907, leaving him with two small children. Laban did not soldier on as a single parent. Few men, especially Europeans, would have in those days. The children went to Martha's mother. The next three years of Laban's life are hazy. Rumors place him in Italy for at least part of that time, in Munich, perhaps at a sanitarium. He essentially dropped out of the society in which he had been involved, and left no tracks.

EVOLVING PHILOSOPHY/CHOREOSOPHY

Laban resurfaced in 1910, after having met his second wife, the singer Maya Lederer. They married and moved to Munich. In Munich, Laban found an "island of international culture ... an oasis of anti-authoritarian thought and easy-going tolerance." (Preston-Dunlop, 1998, p. 17). Munich was café-society in its early stages—cabarets, puppet theaters, balls and soirees. The Blaue Reiter group—consisting of the artists Kandinsky, Klee, Franz Marc and others—promoted a more spiritual and expressive approach to abstract art. The composer Arnold Schoenberg was also in Munich at that time, raising questions about what was harmony, harmonic and harmonious.

Munich was a smaller and more intimate city than Paris and the emerging cabaret and cafe scene provided a locale for writers, artists, musicians and performers to share their concerns about the wealthy and the bourgeoisie. The artists sitting around in cafés were against rigidity of thinking, status-driven success, hypocrisy and complacency. They produced magazines, newspapers, paintings, small theatrical events, vaudeville-like performances, atonal music, and more in the service of the nouveau.

Laban's movement influences during this period also included the body-culture approaches of Bess Mensendieck, Rudolf Bode and Emil Jaques-Dalcroze, all of whom were part of the physical, spiritual and expressive culture-of-the-whole that was prominent in Munich at that time. He studied Noverre's *Letters on Dancing and Ballet*, a text from the eighteenth century in which Noverre recommends privileging the storyline of a ballet over the decorative and technical prowess of the time. Laban was aware of the notation systems used in historical dance forms (especially Feuillet notation, with its swirling pictorial pathways that so well represent Baroque dance). Between Feuillet and Noverre, Schoenberg and Kandinsky, and Dalcroze and Bode, the intertwining of threads into a new dance theory was set to begin. Laban was ready to begin weaving these threads.

COMMUNING IN ASCONA

It was in the summer of 1913, just before the world changed forever, that the evolving artist/researcher/visionary/philosopher Rudolf Laban watched a young woman trudge up the hill towards him. She had walked, carrying her suitcase, from the town of Locarno (near the border between Switzerland and Italy) to the village of Ascona. Her name was Mary Wigman, and she was climbing the hill to participate in a community experiment in expressive dance. The hill, called Monte Verita, or the Mountain of Truth, was inhabited by a collection of painters-turned-dancers, singers-turned-actors, dancers-turned-lovers ... in short, what the 1960s labeled "hippies."

Laban had been invited to open up a summer school for the arts in Ascona. He had only recently abandoned his visual art training and identity for that of a dancer/movement artist. Up to this point Laban had not taken an interest in the politics of communal living or anarchy, both of which were of concern to the Asconans. Only the unconventional nature of his relationships with his wife, the singer Maya Lederer, and his mistress, the Dalcroze-trained dance teacher Suzanne Perrottet, indicates a connection to the free-loving founders of the Ascona community. But he understood the mysticism, the triangular balance of Love–Work–Play that had emerged as a cornerstone of the Asconan philosophy.

Ascona is a little village off the beaten path of any of the deep historical struggles in which most of Europe was engaged at the time. It had been re-founded as a utopian and anarchical community in 1900.

According to Martin Green, author of *The Mountain of Truth*:

> At the end of the nineteenth century, intellectual Europe became preoccupied with the problem of its own unhappiness, malaise, or—to use Freud's word—Unbehagen. The favorites of this rich and powerful civilization—the economically and educationally privileged, the most intelligent and imaginative—felt themselves to be unhappier than more primitive peoples. All over Europe … the Germans and German-speaking … were moving faster than other peoples to grasp the glittering prize of progress.

(Green, 1986, p. 1)

But the "glittering prize of progress" lost its burnish with the loss of the direct experience of the world. At the same time, a longing for Community had taken over. The Industrial Revolution had separated man from his produce, and had objectified the experience of "making." Therefore, many intellectuals and sociopolitical people felt the need to withdraw from both the industrialization of the workforce and the science-centered empiricism taking over the academy. They divided what was functional from what was expressive. Living a new life together, in a community in which the needs of the individual might be subsumed to the greater good of the whole, had its attractions.

The Asconans were mystical, but not in a gothic sense. The dark relationships among men were not of interest; instead, they focused on a spiritual life-changing approach to work, love and play. They developed small collectives, but the famous figures who came to Ascona were not there to build one large community. Hermann Hesse, D. H. Lawrence, Otto Gross, Gusto Graser, Mary Wigman and Rudolf Laban were all in Ascona; we do not know which of them may have crossed paths. But whether they met in person, their ideas did mingle at the base of the Mountain of Truth, and the basic philosophy resurfaces even today.

Community was an emergent rather than an ideological notion. The cohorts that developed were small and not possessive of ideals or of property. Ascona was a "seed community" in every sense of the word. Growing organically was a metaphor for the way small groups grew up and were reaped and divided and reseeded. These themes played out in the spontaneous dances that arose and were refined during Laban's Ascona period.

Other dancers, in addition to Wigman who came to work with Laban on Monte Verita, included Kathe Wulff, a visual artist; Sophie Tauber, a painter (later married to Jean Arp, the Dadaist artist); Laura Oesterreich, a trained dancer; his wife the opera singer Maya Lederer; his mistress Suzanne Perrottet; and a young dark beauty named Betty Baaron Samao (Preston-Dunlop describes her as the children's nanny, but she appears in dance photos and seems to be a lovely dancer). The confluence of various art forms with the ideas of free love, feminism, organic gardening and freemasonry led to explorations of new forms of creating and sharing dance.

In this maelstrom of influences, Laban evolved methods based on spontaneous processes and an overall sense of design. The result was something he eventually called "Movement Choir." Drawing on improvisational impulses, musical theory and visual design structures, this form was devised and spontaneous, participatory and performative. It was contemporaneous produced and particular folk dance, with contributions from each individual and a resultant communal sense of identity.

Mary Wigman came into this scene after having been disillusioned by the Hellerau (Dalcroze-based) community's emphasis on music over movement. She arrived in time to begin to working with Laban's approach, which she had been told was the dance-centric process she was seeking.

The group's second summer at Ascona, in 1914, began with plans for clarifying the triad of concepts Laban was developing: Tanz, Ton, Wort (Dance, Sound, Word). But weeks into the process, the outbreak of World War I shattered this creative Garden of Eden. It is difficult for us now, looking back after almost a century has passed, to comprehend how devastating it was in the summer of 1914 to have the world (or Europe) rocked by simultaneous declarations of dissolution and nationalism. To the Asconans, whose community was built upon crossing traditional boundaries, and balancing forces of opposition, the loss was devastating. Most returned to their native countries, to try to live within the national boundaries they had tried to transcend. But Laban and Wigman stayed, keeping the Garden of Eden open precariously until October, when the cold weather forced their return to the crumbling civilizations of Europe.

During the war, Laban traveled between Munich, Zurich and, occasionally during summers, Ascona. A good deal of work on the idea of notation happened during this time, and there was much correspondence between Laban and Suzi Perrottet about the theory of movement analysis. Laban drew inspiration from all of the women in his life: Mary Wigman, Maya Lederer and Suzanne Perrottet. In his letters to Suzi, who was often in Zurich while Laban was in Munich or Ascona, he told her what he was experimenting with. "What if I take music away from dance?" he asked.

Wigman had left Hellerau and Dalcroze over the same question. In their work together, Laban and Wigman worked to free dance from music. At one point during the war, he asked Wigman to take over his teaching duties in Zurich while he recuperated from one of his many episodes of illness. Most of these episodes were intestinal, with regular bouts of depression, and he often had to ask students to step into the role of instructor. Wigman moved into a flat above the studio and together they began to derive a curriculum for training dancers. They created a basis for Choreutics (Space Harmony) and Eukinetics (Effort); a theory they developed in order to clarify technique and style and in order to move beyond dance steps into meaningful movement. Together they were laying the groundwork for a new approach to modern dance; one that was expressive of Mother Nature and human nature, that embraced the outer and the inner terrain, and contained the fundamentals of movement: changing, shifting and adapting tensions.

Laban began to write a book (*Die Welt des Tanzers*) and to articulate his vision for a new approach to dance based in theory, practice, experimentation, community and access to basic elements, with dance as an art form in and of itself.

Despite the brutality of the war, Laban held on to some utopian ideals of community and crossing artistic, moral and geographic boundaries. For at least one month (March 1915) Maya, Suzi, Laban and Wigman all lived together in a farmhouse. Maya and Suzi were both pregnant by Laban at the same time. Laban's philosophy of living an essential and organic lifestyle and his generous and bemused approach to the women in his life fostered a sense of the communal over the materialistic. He came and went, from the farmhouse, from Maya's house in Munich and Suzi's in Zurich; he worked with Wigman in Ascona. The art always came first.

Antja Kennedy (Interview, July 8, 2004) pointed out that Laban was an autodidact, keeping his own counsel. No one could tell him he was a bad choreographer or criticize him in any way when he was doing his experiments on the hillside in Ascona. But despite the fact that Munich was a hotbed of experimental art, especially painting and sculpture, it was much tougher to break into the more traditional venues with new ideas about dance. Munich had an opera house, with the standards and traditions that accompany an established artistic domain. In writings at the time, Laban hinted that he did not necessarily want critical eyes observing his early work. After all, movement choirs were made by and for the people who were dancing them, and they were experiments, not products. He was thinking big, and beginning to produce something quite new. The staid opera houses of Europe were not the place for his explorations.

LEARNING FROM THE WORLD

Evelyn Dörr (Interview, July 9, 2004) described Laban's philosophical explorations during the war and post-war period. "He is looking at ethnology, psychology, physiology, folk, research, philosophy: the symbol of the Creation, nature and Christianity, changing and symbols of the libido, and archetypes." She believes he had questions about Darwinism; wondering if society is based on a hierarchy designed in part by nature. She said that Laban seemed to be evolving a new and systematic way for seeking unity in nature and the place of the human in the universe, through the study and practice of dancing.

Other influences on Laban's evolving theory included the then-popular notion of naturally occurring symmetry in both nature and art, and the idea of a shared symbology in dreams, a la Jung. Laban utilized such ideas in developing the early symbols for notation, which were imagistic. Laban attempted the alchemical in his notation system: he was trying to capture the very nature of change.

The revolutionary and evolutionary theory Laban constructed led to dance practice that was the meeting ground for the participatory and the expressive, the inner and the outer experience of the world, the intrinsic and the communicative, thought and action—in short, the field upon which mankind engages with the world of objects and of fantasy, truth and beauty, imagination and experience, and the body moving in space.

POST-WAR RECOVERING

In the years immediately following World War I, Laban found himself with a number of children (by 1917, he had sired eight), an open marriage, followers, colleagues and a fairly transient lifestyle. Maya and her children were in Munich; Suzanne and their son in Zurich, and his children with Martha Fricke were in Hanover, with her family.

Teaching and lecturing in both Zurich and Munich, he became caught up with the Dadaists and the Cabaret Voltaire scene, and began to make chamber dance works. These works were created in a studio setting (in Zurich), but lacked the short, disconnected, improvised bursts of phrases, repeated over and over, that characterized Dada dance performances. While Wigman had begun her own explorations of dark passions, Laban explored archetypal characters who wandered through movement narratives with unconventional encounters.

However, like the Dadaists, he was searching for new choreography forms from an extreme direction. He wrote that "all the big-headed of the world have sent their main people to Zurich" (Dörr Interview, July 9, 2004). But his revolution was different from theirs. He was a rule breaker, a liberalist, and a positivist, according to Evelyn Dörr, and he was more of a reformer than a nihilist.

Many in post World War I Europe became fascinated by the emerging sciences and explored the connections between experimental science and philosophical thought, between psychology and art, seeking to unveil the essences of each. Laban, too, was concerned with all of the facets of analysis of the world of objects and visible phenomena, and he was beginning to articulate, even to lecture about a new psychophysical organization of the body in movement, which he understood to be grounded in both rhythm and space.

PUBLISHING AND THEORIZING IN STUTTGART

After Laban moved to Stuttgart for a time right after the war, he worked further on the analysis of spatial tensions, or pulls, and began to draw symbols for these lines of movement or inclinations off the vertical.

One of the people who came to study at the school in Stuttgart was a young man named Kurt Jooss. Jooss described himself as "entirely unsuited to be a dancer." But, he went on, "from the first moment of being in this new world ... a complete change overtook me. I became deeply involved, my body changed, and my whole being became gradually part of this art" (from the Jooss exhibition catalog, quoted by Partsch-Bergsohn and Bergsohn, 1973, p. 19).

The city of Stuttgart embraced Laban's work and the city of Mannheim followed suit, hiring him as a guest choreographer to make a new production of *Tannhauser*. He wanted to do well because he needed ongoing work, but he also wanted to reform dance itself, to make the artificial more real. More real meant more organic and less mired in traditional dance steps and techniques. As much as he admired Noverre and the dances of the Baroque era, he wanted at this point to break new ground and produce work appropriate to the rising human spirit of the everyday.

His approach was not procedural or systematic; it was inspired. He wanted to provide accessible egalitarian art that connected human beings to their own mythologies and resolutions. And so he became an active teller of stories through tanztheater: dance theater stories told as cautionary tales that also contained prescriptions for transcendence and awakenings.

Laban was set back by a bout of the Spanish Influenza in 1919, an episode which only contributed to his long-term health problems and difficulties earning money on a regular basis. As a Hungarian, he was essentially stateless following the changing borders post World War I. In addition, a new relationship with the Russian dancer, Dussia Bereska, led to the total breakdown of his home life, such as it had been, so he was homeless as well. Although he did not divorce Maya until 1925, after 1918 the marriage was essentially over. Maya was a most understanding ex-wife; Suzi, a most understanding ex-mistress.

Wigman, too, was an understanding ex-pupil, at least for a while. Her work was receiving increasing attention, she was fully German in the eyes of those who cared about such things, and she was a bolder and more singular artist than Laban. While he was interested in the group experience, Wigman was developing her own choreographic voice, primarily as a soloist. Both were leaders and visionaries, but

Wigman described Laban at the time as "the worshipped hero." She had to move on and find her own place.

LABAN AS PERFORMANCE-PRACTITIONER

Meanwhile, Laban developed two approaches to creating the type of dance works he was interested in making. On the one hand, he created dance theater works based on archetypes and fantastical stories, using dancers he trained in his global approach to movement. This was the Tanzbühne Laban, the Dance-Theater group, and a smaller version developed in 1923, the Kammertanzbühne Laban, or Chamber Dance Group. He created the first Tanzbühne in 1920, with his new partner, Dussia Bereska, in Stuttgart. He also further developed the communal, improvisational and participatory style of the Movement Choir during the 1920s.

Laban had moved to Stuttgart because the city offered him work, but also because his publisher was there. His book, *Die Welt des Tanzers* (*The World of the Dancers*), which he had been working on since 1916, had been ready for publication for most of the war years. But until the war was over, no one was able to gather and edit photographs. The book reveals a great deal about Laban's emerging philosophy of the art form of dance:

Dancing means overcoming indolence. Thus it does not flatter one of man's basic instincts. Dancing also brings release and I personally believe that man has crossed the threshold where indolence prevails over the desire for freedom and light, everywhere in each individual, but in the majority of people there is a dancer—a dancer who wants to be released.

The final aim. If the result, namely the extinction of a great number of habitually accepted ideas, feelings, and actions is achieved, then there shall be space for knowledge and function which meanwhile has been developing.

Only then shall we be able to speak of the coming transference of the pure reason expressed in the dance to human life.

(Laban, 1920, translated by Richard Schröder)

The ideal of "pure reason" expressed through the art of dance permeates Laban's writing and thinking from *Die Welt des Tanzers* forth. He saw himself as both an artist and a researcher (or what we might now think of as a social scientist). Science, philosophy, religion and art were spokes on a wheel, ways of understanding the nature of humanity. Dance reflected all of it and was a part of advancing that understanding.

Laban perceived movement primarily as transformation or change. He was concerned with irregular pulls, constantly shifting sands, crystals, vectors and parabolas, psychology, and mapping constant modifications of movement. His earliest forays at creating a notation system consist of shapes that are reminiscent of vectors in geometry—displacements from the vertical, according to Jeffrey Longstaff, a Laban Movement Analyst in Britain. His wedding of mathematics and art, physics and human movement was both of his time and prescient. By the time the notation system we now know as Labanotation was developed, it was a much more static and simple graphic representation of movement qualities, attitudes and directions. But what Laban was playing with in the late 1910s and early 1920s looks more like something in a paisley design.

The 1920s were a rich period of creative development for Laban. They also revealed some tensions among his followers. He developed the notation system, not as a static plotting of positions of body parts but as a way to capture the shifts off the vertical, the sweeping or coned tracks of movement in ever-changing spatial configurations. He was exploring and attempting to "capture the eternal in time and space" (a description of Laban's work by the psychologist Dr Irene Champerknowne, from notes at the Dartington Archives). He was breaking new ground. Not everyone understood, including the critics. The increasingly differentiated paths of Wigman, Kreutzberg, Jooss, Knust, and others, tugged at the German dance world.

In 1921, Laban became the Ballet Master to the national Theater of Mannheim; and he created several works, including *Die Geblendeten*, *Epische Tanzfolge* and the *Orgy of Tannhäuser* by Wagner. He had position and influence in the world of dance. Now he needed the dancers to fulfill his vision.

He began to train his own dancers more methodically by 1923, and set about developing schools and training programs throughout Germany and Switzerland, and eventually, Serbia, Italy and Austria. It was in these schools that the dance and movement choir "curriculum" evolved. Laban was interested in "freie tanz"—dance that was both expressive and highly evolved. The spiritual part of his thinking led him to begin creating tanztheater pieces based on mythical stories and mystical themes. These were performed by trained dancers: small ensembles of eclectic performers who had come to believe in the principles and process Laban was evolving for making compelling and innovative work.

According to Valerie Preston-Dunlop, the chamber groups (tanzbühne) differed from the choirs in several ways. The purpose of the choirs was, in part, to be inclusive and to encourage active participation. The theater works performed by the chamber groups were intended for audiences. The content of the theatrical pieces focused on creating illusion and on social commentary.

Occasionally, the chamber groups and the movement choirs were combined as principles and corps, often for financial reasons: he didn't have to pay the corps. The movement choirs were well-trained bodily, and fulfilled the purpose of supporting the stories with clarity and economy.

In 1923, Laban established the Zentralschule (Central School) Laban and a department for the movement choirs in Hamburg. Among the new dancers who were trained in Hamburg were Ruth Loeser, Sylvia Bodmer, Aino Siimola (later Kurt Jooss' wife), Martin Gleisner and Gertrud Snell.

The choreographic works Laban created between 1923 and 1927 for the Kammertanzbühne Laban include *Der Schwingende Tempel* (*The Swinging Temple*), *Faust Part II*, *Prometheus*, *Die Gaukelei*, *Casanova*, *Don Juan*, *Die Nacht*, *Narrenspiegel* and *Ritterballet*. Specific movement choir works include *Lichtwende*, *Agamemnon's Tod*, *Dämmernde Rhythmen* and *The Titan*.

The curriculum of the Hamburg School contained two tracks, one for chamber groups and one for the movement choirs, but both tracks taught Choreutics (Space Harmony) and Eukinetics (later, Effort). The primary difference between the two tracks was that the choir trained in the evening and weekends, while the chamber group (the Kammertanzbühne) trained daily.

The movement choirs were amateur groups, everyday people who came to the training programs to address growing concerns about the human being within the state, the role of spirituality within religion, and the role of the psyche within the forces at play in the 1920s. Adult students took classes that explored expanding and condensing, individual and group consciousness, breath and story, space (Choreutics) and expressivity (Eukinetics).

As the chamber group traveled around, performing such pieces as *The Swinging Temple*, *Orchidee* (a solo by Dussia Bereska), *Don Juan* and a little piece of structured improvisation called *Die Grünen Clowns* (*The Green Clowns*), Laban pulled in the movement choirs in any given town to augment the ensemble. Since he was evolving his notation system at the same time, the vocabulary he was developing for space and body actions was useful in conveying some semblance of structure in advance. Using this language, he could give some directives, to which the choir members would contribute their own continually refined voices, or personal style. When the performances occurred, the result was always specific and unique. In the case of *The Green Clowns*, for example, (according to Valerie Preston-Dunlop, who has recreated the work), the sequences and the number of dancers changed from town to town, depending on who was available.

Laban was finding some singular threads, some universality in the ways that people learned, presented and experienced dance. In *A Life for Dance*, he wrote about the movement choirs' simple beginnings, in the small towns of Germany in the 1920s:

> We soon got the impression, which was reinforced by our occasional audiences, that we should show our compositions to the public, for nearly everyone who watched us was stimulated into joining in. Meanwhile, our plays had developed into small choir-works. One of the first was Dawning Light, in which we experienced the change from stepping in subdued sadness to the awakening of the revitalizing capacity which is dormant in the body. I emphasize "experienced" and not "presented" because at this stage we had no wish to show or convince an audience—although later on a presentation style emerged effortlessly and without our doing. We were solely concerned with experiencing in ourselves and in togetherness the increased vigour of the spiritual-emotional-physical forces which are united in dance. Why? Because we were drawn to it, we benefited from it, and we were inspired by it.
>
> (Laban, 1975, p. 155–6)

The Tanzbühne group (dance-theater) during the 1920s included Dussia Bereska, with whom Laban had a daughter. (The daughter, named "Little Dussia", was adopted out to a presumably more stable family.) Kurt Jooss, Herta Feig, Jens Keith, Edgar Frank and Albrecht Knust were also a part of the group. The pieces that Laban choreographed in the early 1920s (several of which included the movement choir groups) utilized archetypes and had a mystical flavor. Titles such as *The Fool's Mirror*, *The Crystal*, *Orchidee*, *The Magic Garden*, *The Earth* and *The Titan* reveal Laban's concerns with the imaginative, the socio-political, the natural world, the mythical and the magical.

By the end of the 1920s, Laban and his followers were engaged in coalescing his theories into mutually-informing macro and micro concepts. They perceived the union of opposites along a continuum. They connected form and content, individual and cultural style, sweeping huge ideas into personalized dance stories.

His approach to choreography incorporated all of the theory and practice he had evolved. He wrote about something he called tanzlogisch (dance logic). In his book *Choreographie* (1926) he laid out (p. 89) a sequence of directions that he called a Reihung, a conglomeration of phrases of movement that built up to a scale, like a musical scale, with logic, interval and pattern. He wrote about Formgebilde (what we might now call shape-shifting), which, when done by the dancer's body, is carried into moving through space and thereby delineates the space. It does not matter which parts are moving in order to create the shape because what is essential is that the shape-changing matches the content and spirit of the dance. A single shape can be a headstand or some other position, but it is the sequencing of shapes that matters to the meaningfulness of the dance. One has to lead into another in order to make sense, and that shifting is tanzlogische.

Laban recommended specifying the first shape or point of departure through his emerging symbol system. To him, a true tanzdichter (dance-poet) had to determine if it was important that particular parts of the body were used or if any choice was possible, as long as the intention of the movement was fulfilled. He compared choreography to exploring fingering in piano, with the same sense of craft as well as exploration.

In order to clarify the intention of a movement, the choreographer could use an adjective or adverb to modify and make the movement more expressive. Laban was ahead of his time in his understanding of both effortful and harmonic movement. While many of the European choreographers of this period worked with natural breathing rhythms, and ebb and flow, Laban was more of an architect. For him, natural harmony and design superseded technical prowess.

THE END OF PERFORMING

In 1926, Laban fell off the stage while performing *Don Juan*, and severely injured his back. According to Martin Gleisner (*Laban Art of Movement Guild Magazine*), Laban had created the piece to the music of Glück. The choreography was simple, with group passages danced by students of his schools in the localities of the performances. Gleisner made a case for the professional proficiencies of these students, especially the Jena and Weimar movement choirs.

In February and March, Laban came to Jena to prepare the group for his new work. They rehearsed in the evenings, and Laban worked with Gleisner during the day. Gleisner said he later found Laban's notes on *Don Juan*, but these seem to have disappeared.

By 1926, the movement choirs were quite good, although some were seen as too strict and some as too loose. The Jena movement choir Gleisner oversaw was neither, and held up well in reviews of the piece at the time.

REVIEW OF *DON JUAN* TAKEN FROM *DIE DEUTSCHE FRAU*, NOVEMBER 1926 (TRANSLATION BY RICHARD SCHRÖDER)

While there are still doubtful questions concerning the surprising development of physical awareness which at the moment is very popular, a new German art has matured apart from these misunderstood attempts at rejuvenation and renewal. Whoever has observed the course of development of German dance art only during the last three years could have become confused as to the meaning of this artistic event through the many complexities of its development. But now that Rudolf von Laban has reached the peak with a performance of "Don Juan" in Berlin one may in retrospect be pleased at the resoluteness with which this pioneer has proceeded to open up a new door to artistic expression for the German spirit.

The powerful impression of the performance can only be compared with the experience of hearing Mozart's music for the first time, which went far beyond the trifling rococo, beyond the slightly grotesque distortion of the text, and in its devastating sequence of sound illustrated the dramatic power of the story of humanity. To me the most significant thing about this piece of music by Mozart has always seemed to be that it raised the dramatic experience above mere sensuality and emitted a peculiarly active intellectuality, which made the Faust-like insatiable urge for life out of the countless adventures of the Spanish Knight.

In the darkness of the National Stage in the Bülowplatz the same bewitching experience repeated itself in all the wonder of something seen for the first time. The music by Glück, a few borrowed ballet forms by Angolini provided the vibrant framework, then it suddenly became very clear, which had never happened before, that the strict chamber music of Glück can unite with the dance of the present.

And this is not a marvel because the German Baroque is something other than the florid art of other nations and countries. On it is based the tradition of the religious search for form, bursting vitality and the urge for infinite perspective. Certainly this depth in Glück's string orchestra is primly and reservedly confined. But what unfolds there within the scope of the stage causes sparks to fly from these rhythms, and precisely because of the musical background lacks any over-strong accent, the important things are left for the melody of movement which yonder unfolds before the curtains which suggest only a few symbols.

Triflingly sweet, strongly related to the ballet of the Baroque era, the introduction, the four companions of Donna Elvira and then she herself. Then suddenly the knight disguised as a priest, coaxing and blessing the girls, the untouchable virgin retreating from him instinctively.

Quite quickly the wooing and transition take place, the appearance of Comthur, the fight, the outcome and Elvira's lament. The knight takes his victim away from her father's corpse, Donna Elvira, no other, and then after a passionate dialogue, the development of which is entirely incumbent upon the dance figure, holds only a dead woman in his arms.

And although in these parts of the dance drama entrusted more to the individuals there are moments of compelling greatness, the weight of the artistic experience is felt when the group comes into its own. It now takes over the action of the drama, its powerful ability to express intensified by the varied and yet uniform resoluteness of the movement. It surges in Dionysian pleasure around the dark knight who stays in the midst of this crowd of exuberant admirers, the romantic hero who never gives himself completely but the intellectual who when drinking deep from the intoxicating cup is always master of his passion and master of the one who submits to him. In this wonderful spirited gesture Laban had also as a contrast to the choir surging round him a few quite great moments. A brilliant idea caused him to make the Moor the opponent, he is a creature of habit, instinct, the slave of baser passions and in his grotesque leaps and wild contortions the dark background for the mastery of the hidalgo

Then comes the third act introduced by a very daring silent scene. The Bacchanal with the knight in the middle storms towards the burial place of the murder victim and behind the palely illuminated crosses rise the shadows of Comthur and his daughter. Here they are met by the loud challenge of Don Juan, here for the first time Comthur grasps the mortal hand, which, however, pulls away from the demonic grip. Only now does the choir change. It becomes a host of hellish messengers, who surround the outlawed one like red waves and drive him from one corner of the proscenium to the other. Still, invincible mortal defiance rebels against the annihilating forces—until once again Comthur appears and pulling the evildoers to him sinks down with him. The choir however, with hands waving triumphantly over their heads, engulfs them like a red glow.

Our pictures have captured a few moments of the play. As good as the performance is it must also be added that the picture can no more do justice to the dance than word can reproduce the expression of the dance because these pictures capture only a second of motionlessness in the course of the movement which actually is not there. The real expression is in the sequence, in the course, in the lively arabesque, in the flow of the line, which in intensification contain the climax, in the greatest degree of force the relaxation. They are means of expression that we are only now learning to use again after they had faded in the last offshoots of the court ballet, which on its way to great art became fixed and finally was only the expression of sensual pleasure. *This newborn German dance spans the whole cycle of life. It is nothing less than the expression of a new universal feeling. It embraces universal heaven and hell and on its horizon is dawning the infinity of all living things.*

The review shows both the level of celebrity Laban had achieved, not only for himself, but for dance in Germany and the depth of understanding the writer had for what Laban was trying to do in movement and theater. His ideas had come to fruition in noticeable and effective ways, and his creative work had risen to the level of his theoretical work. He moved people.

There are few accounts of what happened on the night he fell. Apparently, Don Juan was supposed to step backwards off the stage and fall onto a mattress. Some accounts say the choir threw him off the stage, missing the mattress completely; others say he simply overshot the mark.

He never performed again, but found ways to continue to lead the dance field through teaching and evolving his theoretically informed artistry. He toured Europe, lecturing and demonstrating his ideas about notation, dance for the layman, dance training and scientific bases for human movement analysis.

THE APPROACHING NIGHTMARE

Laban's work became darker, at least in the case of *Die Nacht*, in 1927. He describes the source of the work as the visits he had made to the stock exchanges of Paris some twenty years earlier:

> I … watched the excited jobbers pushing and shoving in and out, with fixed stares on their faces, shouting hoarsely and brandishing bits of paper. They would tear these out of each others hands, career madly about and then collapse in despair in a heap, only to shoot off again, hunting for yet another piece of paper … I got to know the ugliness of the class struggle … I went eagerly to meetings … where I could see waves of hatred being artificially generated and becoming so real that they were almost physically hanging in the air. …
>
> A vision took shape within my mind: a dance of the eternally hurrying ones, a dance of the rootless, a dance of the sick cry for the longing of lust, a dance of alluring, seductive women, a dance of greed, a chaotic quivering accompanied by crazy laughter.
>
> (Laban, 1975, pp. 41–42)

The timing of his disquiet is significant; the piece was done as the greed of the 1920s was heading towards its peak, just before the rise of Adolf Hitler. Hitler and the Nazis promised solutions to the dissolute pursuit of money and sex, and that aspect would certainly have appealed to Laban's own concerns.

The work he created in 1927 was not a success, but it was, according to Valerie Preston-Dunlop (1998, pp. 128–129), a shocking piece. Laban explained:

> The play opened with a crowd of mechanically grinning society men and women, followed by all I had experienced and felt when I first met life in the

big city. ... Greed, covetousness, adoration of three idols: dollars, depravity and deceit ... It is always tragic when people can no longer laugh at the maze in which they are lost. But also in my play the happy ending was missing. Who could have dared to hope for this in those days?

(Laban, 1975, p. 43–45)

The first Dancer's Congress and Theater Exhibition in Magdeburg also took place in 1927. It was at this event that the growing tensions among the German dance leaders surfaced for all to see.

The Congress revealed a friction among those who valued ballet (Kröller), those who used combined forms (Laban and Jooss) and Wigman, who was decidedly modern.

Heinrich Kröller (1880–1930) was a German ballet master and choreographer.

A secondary conflict was over a proposed high school for dance with subsequent arguments over the content and approach of the school. On the positive side, Laban's notation system was welcomed by all, especially by Jooss. But there was also a lack of communication and organization, described by Valerie Preston-Dunlop as "problematic" (1998, p. 125). The Theater Exhibit was apparently a nightmare of dysfunction. Wigman was not included. She was also given conflicting information about a performance schedule, and she apparently announced at the end of a performance that she was disbanding her company due to financial concerns. While the committee members, who had tried to bring everyone together (including Oskar Schlemmer with his Bauhaus dances) soldiered on, the tensions were never really resolved. Although the differences among the German "founders" became abundantly clear, and despite the disagreements and financial concerns, the Congress was also another step in Wigman's process of establishing herself as, at the least, Laban's equal, and no longer his pupil.

ADVANCING MASTERY

In 1929, Laban was asked to choreograph a festival in Vienna. The situation was already politically charged: the craft guilds that were to be a part of the parade were separate little cultures. The financial situation that year was dire. People were fearful of the future, which caused some consternation among the planners, who were determined to avoid dissension while promoting the industries. The members of the guilds themselves were concerned that the visiting choreographer would have them hopping as they paraded along. They did not want to hop.

Laban set about to learn the movements inherent in each craft. He learned how to shoe horses, how to trim flowers, how to make pottery, etc. He took each of these work-dances and devised short choreographed pieces based on the essential patterns, both functional and expressive, of each guild. The results went far beyond expectations. It was an event that reminds us of the true value of Laban's contributions to dance and to the world. Laban wrote that the performers thanked him, because in the course of performing their work-dances, they had "fallen in love with their work again" (Laban, 1975, p. 143). They each understood what only the masters of the craft knew: that the essence of the movement was the essence of the craft.

In 1929, he was also lecturing, including a series of talks on the "Problems of Dance" (Maletic, 1987, p. 13–14). Laban laid out the categories to be addressed in dance as separate but interconnected modes of the field. His approach to dance for laymen (the first of the categories) reflected the need for essence and authenticity, even in quotidian play and interactions, while the scientific approach to dance analysis (the second category) included three areas: choreosophy (aesthetics), choreology (analysis of space and time) and choreography (notation). The art of dance, or what had evolved from the tanztheater and expressive dance works was the third category, and dance pedagogy was the fourth. Such categories did not diminish Laban's understanding of the world of dance, rather, they refined and clarified what he had begun to delineate from the all-encompassing free expressivity of Ascona. But the process of demarcation created yet another tension: his desire to release the human spirit from boundaries of time and place, while teasing apart the characteristics of time and place.

GROWING DANCE THEORY

By 1930, Laban was feeling the tension between nationalism and socialism that was beginning to increase all around him. His concerns about a loss of human feeling and connection to the work product were not limited to industry. In an article in the journal *Singchor und Tanz* (Mannheim, 15 January, 1929, Vol. II, p. 561), entitled "The Renewal of the Movement in Theater", he wrote about dancing and spirit. He said that theater had abandoned art. He saw a strong attempt to renew or to develop the spiritual part of theater and raised the question: So how can one develop that part?

> It is necessary that every performer masters body and soul. In order to achieve that goal, it's not sufficient to just do rhythmical gymnastics. There has to be an independent dance director in theaters in order to have good results. Young actors/performers should only be allowed to get onstage when they have achieved that mastery in movement. It cannot be some unrelated form. Gymnastics, sports and fencing can be done; it's OK, but they are just not sufficient to transport the spirit of the dance into the theater.
>
> The director of the movement must understand that it's not ok to just take care of the single performer. In order to serve that spirit of dance, one must serve the whole play. There is no theater that has that kind of director now. It's time and we have to get rid of those obsolete directors.
>
> (p. 561, translated by Sabine Fichter)

In another issue of *Singchor und Tanz*, he directly addressed the dance world in "Choreographie und Theater":

> Dance is a serious art form. Dance now requires further development that goes into more depth. Improvising is not enough—it's not really art. The problem for many dancers is that they have been working as soloists and could not have an objective view on what they do. This is a big problem.
>
> (February, 1929, Vol. IV p. 598, translation by Fichter)

Laban proposed that his research-based approach to creating dance meant a new direction for the art form. His space harmony work made it possible to have a more objective view and his notation system took objectivity and the capacity for research even further. Therefore, he wrote that it was possible every dancer would soon be ready to create his/her own dances and so would be able to reflect on what was created, with opportunity to be critical about form, shape, intention, etc. The logical next step would be that dances could be notated and published to a broader audience and followed by exchanges of feedback, reconstruction and refinement of the work. He suggested considering his proposed objective framework, which allowed everyone to interpret movement individually. Laban compared the process to music:

> The same will happen to dance as music. In general there will be a distinction between those who create and those who will perform those dances. The possibility of notating dances will be something that will be important throughout history and for the future and will be an important step for this genre. That is a problem with old theater pieces that have been done before; we have no written record. This will change now. Poetry and music have been notated and preserved. Only those things that are notated can be taken seriously.
>
> (February, 1929, p. 598, translation by Fichter)

Laban went on to say that "good directors are movement poets." The director's job is to clarify, humanize and preserve dance movement so it can be replicated and still stay alive.

TOSSING AND TURNING

The book *A Life for Dance* was first published in 1935, but Laban wrote it as he struggled with his standing as a choreographer and leader of the German dance world and the hints of coming fascism in Germany. In it, he described his early concerns with class struggles. He asked:

> Why care for the satisfied and wealthy, who build such a pathetic illusion of happiness with farthings snatched ruthlessly from the poorest, while their own souls wither and perish among their gilt and opulence? ... How can true beauty dwell among the glitter of tattered silk and under the artificial purple lights? How can the soul rejoice amid the tattered rags of the poor and hollow-eyed children? How utterly remote is the fragrance of the mountains and forests from the air of the slums, so thick with coal dust ... Is that the song of man?
>
> (Laban, 1975, p. 42–43)

Even as the "song of man" showed early signs of discord, Laban needed income and he sought a position as a ballet-master within the dance world. Many of the ballet companies at that time were affiliated with the opera, and the art form had become stultified. Laban wanted to put his ideas into full practice. When he was appointed to this position, at the Berlin State Opera, in 1930, there was both resistance and curiosity among the dancers. He was not going to support the star system and he was excited about getting the ballet dancers to expand and explore new movement material. Many of the stars of the German ballet companies took exception to his ideas.

The socialist ideals Laban espoused in his book and in his position came up against the Nazis' rise to power in Germany, carried as they were on some of those ideals. Laban was in favor so long as he cooperated with the nationalist agenda.

And he tried to cooperate, for a while. His creative ideals had found support, at least at first. His interest in the mystical and in Wagner's triumphal music has been seen as evidence for his purported manipulative and dictatorial tendencies. Some dance scholars make a case that Laban had a plan for the domination of the world of dance because his work came to be used in a set and stultifying way, in the later Nazi and post-World War II periods.

There is insufficient evidence to support the characterization of Laban as an ambitious tyrant. In fact, the values and behaviors Laban expressed suggest that he was not domineering but seductive; not controlling or rigid but engaged and improvisational. For Laban, dance was the preferred way to address these values. His goal was freedom, light and a new reasoning based on experiencing and interacting dynamically. He was far more interested in the process of opening up and expanding one's personal expressive range than he was in his own personal power or any particular sociopolitical outcome.

Evelyn Dörr put it this way: Laban was focused on themes of being, developing and decomposing/dying. His leitmotif and guiding principles explored symmetry and asymmetry, dynamics, rebounding from sustainment, etc. His work and values went against the Nazi notion of despotism, even if neither he nor they could see the conflict at first. He followed the path of art and humanist movement (Dörr interview, July 9, 2004).

Those who knew Laban best have supported Dörr's contention that Laban was, in essence, naïve. He thought he could influence the Nazis and show them his way was best. The tension he felt was a struggle between his notion of a dance technique that was based in release of ideology, position, or steps, and which he wanted to see housed in a real theater, for audiences to see. The desire to work with the ever-darkening power structures of the Nazis in order to realize his dreams, in contrast with his awareness of the soullessness of any political machine—much less a fascistic one—brings into sharp focus a piece he created in 1927, *The Titan*.

Titan was, in part a piece that arose from his short visit to the United States in 1926. In *A Life for Dance*, Laban offered up his ethnographic analysis of the melting pot of American dance, although the chapter is sprinkled with what we would now recognize as ignorant racism and sexism. He expressed admiration for the "Red Indian" and was less taken with the African–American culture of Chicago at the time (There is a suggestion that he may have been mugged or ripped off by a prostitute there.) His description of his trip reveals naiveté as well as animosity towards certain ethnic groups, if not a tendency towards over-personalization and projection. But he ends the chapter with this:

> The purpose of life, as I understand it, is a care for the human as opposed to the robot; a call to save mankind from dying out in hideous confusion; an image of the festival of the future, a mass of life in which all the celebrants in communion of thought, feeling, and action, seek the way to a clear goal, namely to enhance their own inner light.

> (Laban, 1975, p. 137)

Valerie Preston-Dunlop (1998, p. 127) points out how easily scholars have used Laban's description of the dance-play's "telling of the strength of the common hope which lies in a common will to achieve something better" as evidence of how the Ausdruckstanz (Expressionist Dance) was in tune with Nazism. She goes on to address the concept of the "common," which she points out was a different interpretation of the word from how Laban used it historically. In the movement choir work, there is a common aim—"individual expression through their own light." But that goal does not require a common or regimented approach. Moving together in communion and harmony is not the same thing as marching to a single drummer. And Laban's work required the exercise of the individual artist's mind, body and spirit, in fact demanded a mastery of the discourse of the mind, body and spirit.

In contrast to the Nazi notion of "The Master Race," Laban understood mastery as mastery over self and over mankind's natural indolence. In the end, Laban's definition was too different from that of the Nazis. He understood harmony not as mere structure or regimentation, but as listening, observing and sharing unique aspects, finding common ground that allowed each mover's style to shine and support that of the others.

WAKING UP

In 1932, Laban's former student Kurt Jooss choreographed his masterwork, *The Green Table*. He created it for the Concours International de Chorégraphie en Souvenir de Jean Borlin, a competition organized by the Archives Internationales de la Danse, held at the Théâtre des Champs-Elysees in Paris, in July, 1932. The piece was a huge success. Although he claimed the work was not an anti-war ballet, he was astute enough to see what was happening in Germany. Jooss' wife, Aino, and his composer Fritz Cohen were Jewish and the danger was much clearer to him than it appeared to be to Laban. Jooss warned Laban about the Nazis, and advised him to leave as well. His Jooss Ballet toured for a bit and then settled in southwest England, at an estate called Dartington Hall.

Laban did not leave Germany when Jooss advised him to, and his remaining has led to much speculation and interpretation about the reasons why. There is evidence of cooperation with the National Socialists in regard to delivering lists of Jewish students and in banning, in particular, one Jewish dancer, from observing his work in 1934. Those events happened, but we do not know why he cooperated to the extent that he did. Interviews and readings reveal a range of possibilities, from total naiveté, to coercion by the Nazis, to alleged agreement with the Nazi goals.

He did not join the party, and he was not a fascist, although it is equally clear that he was naively racist, in a passive way, from his writings about the "Red Indian" and Negroes in America. He may have stayed in Germany because his work was there, or because he was not so concerned about the racist aspects of the Nazi regime, or he was a little callow about the growing fascism around him.

Nevertheless, by 1936, Laban was getting the idea. He paid as little attention to politics as he could, but he knew what was happening to the voices of individuals under the national socialist framework. In 1936, Laban had position and income, privileges he had not often enjoyed in his life, and that he thought were worth protecting. Nonetheless, in 1936 as a judge at a dance festival, he balked at awarding a prize to a German dance group over other groups, and decided to award prizes to all participants.

Laban was asked to put together a huge movement choir, *Tauwind*, for the opening of a theater in the week leading up to the Berlin Olympics. In the speech he gave at the final dress rehearsal, he praised the uniqueness of the human body moving in concert with others, expressing the very essence of life:

> We do not need to believe in dogmatic explanations, in philosophical systems or in circumstantial calculations to understand the will of life, which fills our whole being. It upsets our natural harmonic condition if we try to find the first source and the final goal outside ourselves …
>
> What does the faith consist of? What is its essence? We believe in a psycho-physiological way to health and happiness and on this we search for a right functioning of our individual as well as community life. The spiritual vision of the world, and the question of the connection and communication with the life force also finds its natural ground here
>
> (Translation by Laban, 1939)

Joseph Goebbels, the Nazi Minister of Culture and, possibly, Adolf Hitler, observed the rehearsal and speech, so Laban's following thought is all the more significant and telling:

> This work demands from us the utmost devotion and great efforts. With these efforts we do not want to cheat or to overreach anybody, we do not want to make a competition and draw external profits. We do not need to fight each other, or envy the other's possession. We carry all we need within ourselves.
>
> (Laban, 1939)

What Laban expressed is a clear reference to the Asconan ideals of individual and group interdependence, of the organic unfolding within human institutions of community. Goebbels understood the message very well. In his diary, he commented: "It is all dressed up in our clothes and has nothing whatsoever to do with us" (quoted in Preston-Dunlop, 1998, p. 196). The performance was prohibited. He was accused of homosexuality, a denigration that would have cut deeply. His papers were seized, his travel limited. Laban's career in Germany was over.

He tried to stay, sending a letter to a friend, Marie Lieschke, and asking her to speak to some of the Nazi officials on his behalf, but his fate was sealed.

Eventually, he found his way to Paris, a desperately ill and broken man. He planned to stay with Dussia Bereska who was running a dance school in Paris, but, according to some interviewees, she was drinking quite a bit. He ended up in a dark and damp basement room, where his plight came to be known to Kurt Jooss.

RE-ENERGIZING AT DARTINGTON

Jooss, his family and his company had found another little jewel of a location in Dartington Hall, Britain, an old estate that had been purchased by Leonard and Dorothy Elmhirst. The Elmhirsts were an intriguing couple: she was an American, a Whitney; he was an idealistic young Brit. They met at Cornell University and devised a dream between his vision and her money. Their home, Dartington Hall, purchased in 1925, became a center for Leonard's experiments in progressive education, rural "reconstruction" (Leonard's word), and, eventually, a refuge for artists.

At Dartington, a number of artists found a home, however briefly, with the Elmhirsts. The list included Mark Tobey, Bernard Leach, Michael Chekhov, Rabinath Tagore, Cecil Collins, Imogen Holst, Benjamin Britten, Peter Pears, Michael Tippett, the Amadeus String Quartet, Ravi Shankar, Viyhat and Imrat Khan, Stravinsky, Hindemith, Poulenc, Lutoslawski, John Cage—and many more.

Laban arrived at Dartington in 1937, sick and devastated. The students there at the time were told to leave him alone. According to Ann Hutchinson Guest, on occasion he could be spotted in the balcony that overlooked the dance studio, where the Jooss Ballet rehearsed, a figure in shadows.

He might have stayed in those shadows were it not for Lisa Ullmann, one of Jooss' dancers, who became Laban's domestic partner, leading him back into the world, and nurturing both his being and his vision.

It was in his little studio that Laban could be found, studying crystals and thinking about how matter forms itself into beautiful shapes, without consciousness but with a logic based in physics and metaphysics. The swinging scales he had developed some twenty years earlier made sense kinesthetically, allowing the body to fall, as it did, into natural rhythms and directions in space. He began to write and talk about spatial pulls and tensions that lived inside various crystalline forms, and to discover the multi-dimensional ways the human body can transcend gravity and achieve a spicier harmony with nature, one in which movers and environment partner actively and responsibly.

In Ascona, Laban had engaged with the Rosacrucians, the Freemasons and other cult-like groups that also professed openness to seeing the possibilities of human transcendence and a marriage of the spirit and imagination. Laban was not really interested in being part of a cult: he preferred to stand outside and move ideas rather than submit to them. In Southwest England, with time and space galore, he revisited his own thoughts about the myriad ways people are pulled into the farthest reaches of space, orienting themselves to the com-plexities beyond the vertical pull of gravity. He would sit and turn icosahedra and dodecahedra around and around, finding the center and the possibilities in each. And then he would take long walks around the estate, with its fields and sculptures, cows and medieval tilting yard. In the evenings, he and Leonard Elmhirst might sit and talk about farming and human movement, or Laban and Dorothy Elmhirst might discuss the creative work that was as much a product of the estate as the vegetables.

As at Ascona, the Eden-like existence on the Dartington estate was dissolved by war. Once again nationalism and boundaries between governments mattered. As World War II progressed, all German nationals were moved from the coastal regions and the members of the Jooss Ballet were no exception. The Elmhirsts found a farmhouse in rural Wales for Laban and Lisa, and it was here that a young Betty Meredith-Jones studied with them. Betty was a physical educator; she lived in a caravan (trailer, in the USA), while she and Lisa began to decode the theories Laban was garnering from his crystals. Eventually, Betty came to the United States where she pioneered Laban's work in psychiatry and especially with Parkinson's patients.

F. C. Lawrence was a management consultant when Leonard Elmhurst introduced him to Laban. During and after World War II, Lawrence and Laban blended traditional time–motion study approa-ches to worker efficiency with Laban's analysis of effort and space. Observing young women throw around huge tires and pieces of equipment for the war effort gave them opportunities to note the role of personal style in efficiency. Body type and predilections for particular permutations of expression and pathways played a role in the productivity and job satisfaction of the women hired to take over from the men deployed to the war. Laban and Lawrence called their approach "lilt in labour" and it revolutionized industry.

> Few of us realize that our contentment in work and happiness in life, as well as any personal or collective success, is conditioned by the perfect development and use of our individual efforts. We speak about "industrial effort" or "cultural effort", without realizing that each collective action is built up from the mental and manual efforts of individual people.
>
> (Laban and Lawrence, 1974, p. 1)

These same notions of individual style became the basis for Marion North's *Personality Assessment through Movement*, a comparative study of the relationship between individual movement style and classroom behaviors in young children. They also underlay the character development work of Geraldine Stephenson, Yat Malmgren and other teachers of Laban-based movement for actors. Individual style analysis became the seeds for the Action Profiling and Movement Pattern Analysis developed by Warren Lamb, who analyzed the decision-making styles of top team planners in industry.

WINDING DOWN IN MANCHESTER AND SURREY

In 1946, Laban and Lisa established a school in Manchester, called the Art of Movement Studio, with funding from the Elmhirsts. It was here that Valerie Preston-Dunlop, Geraldine Stephenson, Warren Lamb and Marion North, among others, found their life's work. One pupil at the school was a young Joan Plowright. It was Laban who suggested that acting, not dance, might be her forte.

Laban did not teach very often at the Studio, but when he did, the old charisma and vision were apparent. Also apparent were his age and ill-health. The remaining years of his life were full of bursts of creative energy and quick insights, and periods of withdrawal and recuperation.

He fostered the application of his work in several fields. He saw it used in actor training, studies of efficiency in industry, an expanded Labanotation system, early dance therapy/psychiatry and education.

Laban kept an eye on all of it, but he rarely interfered, unless it was to redirect, or in many cases, to tutor or just support a young student.

Geraldine Stephenson describes a moment on a train with Laban, sometime in the early 1950s:

> I was on a train with him coming back from several weeks of teaching various workshops for actors. For some reason, he was with me on this particular trip, but really, I had been doing quite a lot of these by myself. I was just exhausted, and I finally turned to him and said, "I do not think I can go on like this. I need a rest."
>
> He looked at me with his fairly piercing demeanor, and said, "Vat you need to do iss a concert." I was horrified! Here he was, suggesting MORE work, when I needed a vacation! But for some reason, I listened to him, went into the studio for weeks and weeks, and created an evening of solos; short effort studies of characters. This was a big success and led into many other opportunities. He was right. I needed to do something for myself.
>
> (Interview, July 2, 2004)

Many stories abound of his generosity and exacting standards, of brutal reactions, and warm elegance. His former students spoke of his high expectations, the twinkle in his eye, his dark moods, and his spiritual curiosity. For a man whose creative work had been full of social commentary, his political insight was close to non-existent. He had both democratic and anarchical principles, yet he was a stateless person who found himself engaged with nationalism and fascism, in bewildering and sudden juxtapositions.

LOOKING BACKWARDS AND FORWARDS

Rudolf Laban rode along all of the pathways of his times attentively, and with an abiding faith in the nature of the universe to support mankind, even after he saw the limitations and dark nature of mankind. Because he did not plan out his life, or even design his career, he was able to respond to the issues at hand, in the moment, and yet he was also able to avoid taking responsibility for those same issues and in the case of his children, to avoid much more than responsibility. He was an aristocrat who never owned any property, including his own intellectual property, which left his work subject to appropriation, providing a springboard for the careers of others to whom he gave material for further development.

Those who carried the work forward, including Marion North, Valerie Preston-Dunlop, Warren Lamb, Betty Meredith-Jones, Irmgard Bartenieff, Samuel Thornton and so many more, felt empowered to adapt, evolve or augment it in his/her own way. Each adhered to the basic principles of analytic categories, and the basic values of respect for individuality and finding common ground. Interestingly, there was much agreement about those basic principles and values, even though the work looks very different in the hands of those schooled in it by different teachers.

Sam Thornton, who has run summer courses in movement for over thirty years, describes Laban's work with the saying: "We all live in the same world, but we don't all see the same world" (Interview, June 30, 2004).

That statement may best describe Laban's legacy to a world struggling with power, status, greed and war. In terms of politics, while he was not one to comment on government directly or protest policies, he was an astute observer of human conflict.

The Nazi piece is so very tricky however. Artists have historically struggled for approval and funding from those authorized and inclined to provide it. Patronage is a double-edged sword and political hierarchies are real and impact artists. Sometimes the impact is random, sometimes it comes with a vengeance, as in the case of the Nazis, the House Un-American Activities Committee in the 1950s, or the culture wars of the 1990s. The Nazis went after artists for many purported reasons, including a desire to test their loyalties. When Laban's turn to be challenged came, he hastened his exit with the speech he gave before the dress rehearsal of *Tauwind*. He was gone before Kristallnacht as a result of speaking some truth to power. He was not exactly a freedom fighter; but neither was he a despot.

His role was as a social commentator, addressing issues inherently in question during a period of rising fascism. At the same time, he tried to maintain his position within the power structure. In the end, he came face-to-face with bias, unyielding positions, repression and threats, and he chose to escape. For the rest of his life, he struggled with depression and illness, but always came back to the dance itself, for insight, acumen and healing.

In the early 1950s, Laban and Lisa persuaded the Elmhirsts to buy a small estate for the Art of Movement Studio in Addlestone, Surrey. There she taught and he reviewed student work. The studio that was built there was an architectural marvel, and those who studied in it speak of the gardens they helped to nurture alongside their own personal and artistic growth.

Walli Meier, a dance therapist in Britain, tells of her final examination at Addlestone, in which she sat while Laban perused her notations, completed after months of observing psychiatric patients. After turning the pages over and over and scanning, all the while saying "Ja ... Ja ... " he slammed the book shut, chucked it over his shoulder ("All that work!" Walli exclaimed) and looked at her. "Vell, ve know that all, don't ve?" he said. "Now, ve dance!" And so they danced (quoted from a video made by Janet Kaylo and Patrick Lears, May, 1996, from the author's private collection).

Laban took walks and spent time with the cat. He reconnected with his and Suzanne Perrottet's son, Allard, and was devastated when the young man committed suicide. He turned crystals around and learned from them. He drew, he pondered; he made no plans. On July 1, 1958, he died. He is buried in Weybridge cemetery, in an obscure corner, under a headstone that says, simply: "A Life for Dance." The dance lives on.

2

ANALYSIS OF A TEXT, *THE MASTERY OF MOVEMENT*

Laban wrote extensively; in fact, we have more textual material than information about his performance works. From his first grand opus, *Die Welt des Tanzers* (*The World of the Dancers*) to his overview of his theories, *The Mastery of Movement*, to his scribbled notes to himself before his talks, a picture unfolds of a man who put his thoughts on paper in order to explain, portray, describe and illustrate his ideas. On the scraps of paper are bits of notation, drawings, charts, philosophical musings and scenarios.

The opening paragraphs of his 1920 book, *Die Welt des Tanzers*, reveal his overarching purpose in writing about the ephemera of movement:

> As I was about to start my work, to be the first among dancers to speak about a world where language alone is not good enough, I was well aware of the difficulty of this task. Only the firm conviction that one must conquer for the dance the field of literal and linguistic expression in order to gain deserving and very necessary understanding, in as wide a circle as possible, gave me the determination to carry out this difficult and thankless task.
>
> ... Secondly, it is extremely difficult to use the words of our language in such a way that the rare simplicity and yet richness of dancing thought is fully appreciated. Not for nothing does the dancer or his brother in art, the creative artist, remain so often markedly silent, that they are accused of non-thinking.

> Here again only the strong conviction of too much thinking and one-sided thinking is on the edge of the abyss
>
> (Laban, 1920, p. 1)

Laban was familiar with the abyss between theorizing and experiencing the flow of life itself. But he soldiered on, writing and struggling with verbal explanations of a phenomenon both fleeting and deeply encoded in the psyche of each person.

Laban saw theater and dance as not-altogether separate spokes on the same wheel: artistic performance. In the book, *The Mastery of Movement*, he did not differentiate much between character development for theater and rich, clear dance performance. Movement occurs in all forms of performance and it is the clarity and depth of movement with which he was concerned. In fact, the form he wrote about was called tanztheater, or dancetheater. And the goal of the training for the tanztheater was mastery.

In handwritten notes found at the National Resource Centre for Dance (University of Surrey, Guildford, UK) that may have been part of an article on control of performance Laban noted, "We ought to be able to regard regulations as controlling for us those qualities in us which we never really master of ourselves ... The real freedom is the freedom of balance rather than the freedom to go to the devil."

This tension between freedom/flow/innovation and control/containment/regulation of patterns lies at the heart of tanztheater in general, and Laban's approach to performance in particular. Expressionism, or Ausdrucktanz, found fodder in exploring, if not exploiting, such tensions.

During World War I, when Laban and Wigman were working on developing a training curriculum for dance performers, he was taken with the analysis of space, or kinesphere, while Wigman explored the tension and release continuum. Eventually the spatial analysis became the basis for Choreutics, or Space Harmony, and Labanotation, while the tension/release explorations evolved to become Eukinetics, and eventually, Effort analysis.

Ausdrucktanz, the expressionist dance of Germany and Mittleeurope in the 1920s and 30s, celebrated the living human body and spirit at the same time as it abstracted and extended human experiences. Creators of Ausdrucktanz based the work on all forms of performance presentation: human emotions and behaviors were both revealed and commented upon. Exaggeration and repetition, use of quotidian or pedestrian movement, archetypes and contexts turned upside down; all of these are hallmarks of the combination of social commentary and physical spareness and clarity known as the sub-category of Ausdrucktanz that Laban called tanztheater.

For his form of tanztheater, dancers were required to develop a formidable and specific technical proficiency and the ability to perform without artifice or decoration, as a human being or a character who is deeply personal in technique and emotion. The performer's palette of nuanced expressivity was to be highly honed and clarified. Tanztheater style was less about technical virtuosity in terms of the execution of physical steps or actions, and more about precision and intelligibility.

In short, the kind of dance and theater performances Laban was after required mastery of movement as much as the craftsmen of the 1929 Vienna festival parade and the young women tossing huge tires around during World War II required mastery of task. And therefore, he began to write his most explicative book.

The Mastery of Movement was the last book he wrote by himself (although there is no doubt that Lisa Ullmann contributed heavily to both the content and the production of the original text, in 1950). The book was originally titled *The Mastery of Movement for the Stage*, and as such, is the most completely detailed overview of the Laban-based performance work we have from him. He applied his theories to all stage work, which, for him, included both dance and theater. He saw movement study as the "common denominator" and the "common animator" for both.

The book was laid out with a weaving together of theory and practice. In the introduction, Laban stated that he did not set out to write a literary treatise, but rather, to create "an incentive to personal mobility" (p. vi). His invitation went beyond developing the ability to move and to move well. He defined personal empowerment and efficacy through the experience of mastery of movement, as a performer and as a worker in industry.

THE CONCEPT OF POLARITIES UNITED

The concept of "both" rather than "either/or" is introduced early on in the book. Laban went out of his way to explore the notion of polar extremes and the need for integration of oppositional concepts. In all of the theoretical constructions and language therein, opposites are polar ends along a continuum. He described these continua as ways of enriching our understanding of ourselves and what makes us thinking, acting human beings.

He set the tone in the introduction:

> Movement is equally an essential means of artistic expression in drama and in opera; and it is also the means of satisfaction and comfort in situations of work, since movement, when scientifically determined, forms the common denominator to art and industry.

(Laban, 1971, p. vi)

It was, to Laban, the exact experience of moving in the world that provided the common denominator for polar extremes. Art and industry, two separate ways of being in the world, both require movement, to be sure. But it is through movement that the polar extremes inform each other as well.

The first distinction Laban made in the body of the book was between statuary or static art, which he described as that which is remembered and intact in form when one returns to it; and dynamic art, in which the viewer must flow along with the event and perceive in the moment. Through his analysis, he attempted to capture the ever-changing dynamic of the latter forms. To that end, his language of movement included descriptors of ephemeral events, qualifiers and modifiers of actions, which he called "Effort."

EFFORT

"Effort" is the inner attitude towards a motion factor (such as time, weight or focus). The effectiveness of communication (onstage and off) depends upon the conscious choice and range of options of these inner attitudes. For example, Laban used the example of a middle-aged actress *portraying* a young girl, versus *playing* a young girl. The actress who has a range of conscious choices about a variety of attitudinal options can present a performance that is both evocative and true, as opposed to a performance that is artificial.

Laban meant that playing a character is like playing AT a role, or displaying characteristics that do not add up to a realistic portrayal. In another series of notes Laban wrote later, he clarified the difference between portraying and playing. He wrote about an "almost mystical communion with the audience" that can occur when the performer is "dismissed from the bondage of the alien character into which he has been temporarily transformed" (NRCD notes). In other words, portraying a character is more like inhabiting a part of one's self, as opposed to attempting to display disconnected elements of a character.

For the performer, therefore, studying Effort is a journey into the terrain of the internal range of choices each person has, the hidden as well as the outwardly expressed. The goal is to have access to a palette of personally derived and felt attitudes that can be used to tell a story through a truly realized character.

Other notes reveal more musings on this topic of Effort:

> Effort training is not at all without tradition. The age-long cultivation of the art of movement was in its essence always Effort training. It has been split up in the last few centuries into two branches corresponding to the two main social assets which it contains. These two are on the one hand the exhilaration and entertainment resulting from the cultivation of the art of movement and on the other hand the benefit for health, strength and general efficiency resulting from the practice of bodily exercises.
>
> (NRCD notes)

He went on in the notes to speculate on the benefits of Effort analysis to scientists interested in dance and wondered what might be possible, citing the desire for all people to dance, especially with each other, along with the need for people to use the art of movement in industry. It was Laban's purpose to think of Effort as the part and parcel of a range of human activities, each of which could be drawn upon for character development, personal growth and workplace enhancement.

Laban also understood the role of Effort expressivity to ritual and personal style. He reminisced about the days when people learned about ceremony from the viewing of princes and princesses. "Nowadays," he lamented at the time, "we think of ceremony as how film stars light a cigarette."

How a character approaches a ceremonial moment is expressive and revealing of internal attitudes, whether it is lighting a cigarette or entering a room as a princess. Both are functional movements, but also reveal a great deal of information about personality.

In *The Mastery of Movement*, therefore, Laban suggested that performers need to develop a portfolio of expressive choices. Through observation and practice, the palette of possibilities is expanded and deepened.

to develop such a rich Effort life, he wrote, is to study ...ovements. His example was to use the image of a beehive as a source for a city street scene, then to allow the individual aspects of character to emerge from that baseline context.

A group of performers could begin by improvising movement as it might occur on a busy street, keeping the image of a beehive in mind. Specific gestures and interactions would arise that would require each performer to respond Effortfully, thereby creating a palette of characteristic movements that would ultimately, reveal characters.

Once the characters emerge, the specific array of Effort patterns that make up the character can be analyzed for their components.

The four categories of Effort are Weight, Space, Time and Flow. Each category consists of polar extremes of attitudes towards the category:

Weight	Space	Time	Flow
Strong	Direct	Quick	Bound
Light	Indirect	Sustained	Free

These categories are not exclusive of each other; Laban cautioned that living beings manifest complex Effort sequences and ought not be reduced to a single factor of motion. In other words, single Efforts are not entire character descriptors, but appear and disappear in combinations, modifying and shading actions. Character emerges from the baseline patterning of these ever-changing configurations. Such shading produces "more terrific reactions," according to Laban (1971, p. 13). Laban meant that through the exploration of various combinations of Effort characters will be both consistent and clear. In the beehive exercise, above, the personalities would appear from the array of ever-shifting attitudes: for example, a character who arises out of hastening directness might have an encounter with a character who finds that he/she is avoiding the first character and becoming bound and sustained. Dramatic possibilities arise!

Laban wrote that conscious training in what he called "humane Effort" yields a palette "capable of resisting the influence of inherited or acquired capacities." In other words, we are, as humans, capable of transcending the unconscious patterns that we are born with or develop along the way in favor of better patterns; ones that allow us to be more effective in the direction of the greater good. The struggle each of us goes through to develop qualities that are more creditable to mankind is, according to him, drama. Characters struggle with their humanity, just as real humans do, and performers need to engage with their own struggles in order to develop choices as well as to access them.

Therefore, movement training benefits everyday people as well as performing artists. The work, he hoped, goes beyond the merely life-sustaining, or functional. He defined "movement thinking" as a gathering of impressions of happenings that lacks language to orient it to the external world, but which perfects man's orientation to his inner world (1971, p. 17). Movement experiences such as tribal or cultural dances are evolutions of shared characteristics of Effortful rhythmic movement that become markers or identifiers of that culture. Thus, the inner beliefs and outer behaviors manifest in expressive movement that is deeply meaningful.

An example of how a performer might access another culture through Effort is the work of the playwright Athol Fugard, who sets his work in South Africa. The cadences and patterns of the Afrikaaners and the Blacks are different and offer insight into the cultural beliefs and behavioral patterns that his plays explore. Learning the ethnic and cultural movement patterns early in the rehearsal process would unpack a good deal of the meaning within the play.

Continuing this line of thought, Laban pointed out that "Man is the only living creature who is aware of and responsible for his actions." He valued the process of increasing personal ownership of and access to an ever-broadening range of expressive components throughout the book. Laban saw a connection between "movement thinking" and "word thinking" as well, with the goal of continuing reintegration of the self in line with new connections, expressive modalities and learning. Mere imitation of new patterns, he pointed out, does not penetrate the boundaries of the psyche; real learning requires a lively interaction with the possible, a kind of play that is not imitative but intra-active, that allows for mastery of movement.

The actors in a Fugard play, for example, would not only come into "more terrific reactions" through the investigation of the Effort life of the characters, they would also develop insight into their own expressive lives and beliefs, and would expand those as well.

DEVELOPMENT OF STYLE

The choice of the word "mastery" for his text was not accidental. The second part of the book begins with a developmental perspective; particularly emphasizing the process of delineations of flow as increasingly discrete modifiers of action. He pointed out that as the mover develops skills that are both increasingly functional and expressive, he/she also develops more specialized body part usage, temporal phrasing, access to Space and specific uses for Effort. What is unconscious becomes more conscious. As he/she develops and learns, the mover becomes a more nuanced and effective communicator.

The mover develops a particular "STYLE." Style is more than accessing one's preferred patterns and baselines. Laban identified style as grounded in one's own appetites. Each of us values ideals of beauty and utility. We may cook with a flourish, thereby combining function and expression. One can step carefully and with consideration, another rushes in impulsively, another inspires through speech and gesture, etc. It is the combination of that which we value for the purposes of aesthetics, communication, and efficiency that constitutes personal style.

As in most of Laban's thinking, style is also about both the details of a stance or shift—how a hand changes in relationship to the torso, for example—as well as the mover's attitude towards the moment or event. The movement analyst observes at the meta- and micro-levels, noting recurring patterns and sudden innovations as part of the subsequent blueprint to be analyzed.

But the performing artist, he pointed out, cannot stay within his/her own style. "The artist has to represent more than typical styles or typical beauty—he is interested in all the deviations and variations of movement" (Laban, 1971, p. 93). Therefore, an array of styles, as in a library of possible world-views, and with full awareness of how each compares to one's own personal style, belong inside an actor's toolbox, as colors belong on a visual artist's palette.

Laban did not see style as a part of a series of static positions or moments either. Unlike many body language proponents of the latter part of the twentieth century (Julius Fast comes to mind), he understood that the process of **change** within movement reveals far more about personal style than a particular pose or body-part relationship does. Movement is personally and culturally significant, and crossing one's arms does not indicate any particular meaning. Rather, each moment or pose is part of a series of unfolding moments, which relate to the context and inner landscape of the mover, cultural mores, memories and objective.

As an example, for dancers, the ballet positions of arabesque or attitude are too often approached as stationary placements of body parts, without meaning or significance beyond the physical execution of a static pose. He suggested looking at them not as positions, but as results of dynamic movement changes that lead to particular places in space. In the case of the arabesque, for example, rather than the dancer thinking in terms of achieving a particular placement of the leg behind and above the torso, he suggested the dancer feel the lengthening in two directions of the torso and the leg, in a counter-tension. He saw movement occurring in phrases or sentences, groupings of unfolding moments that yield rich information about the body moving expressively in space.

Laban cautioned actors that much of what is conveyed as character and story is conveyed through movement. To dancers, he said that it is the unusual combinations of movement styles and phrasings that make the work interesting. Audiences are drawn to innovation and new patterns, while also recognizing archetypal behaviors.

Ballet, especially, is not necessarily the tool of a dying regime (a la Russia or Louis XIV) but a

> healthy regenerating factor in which way the reawakening of the long for-
> gotten unconscious powers of man ... might contribute to civilasatory [sic]
> advance ... Other civilizations have in any case missed the occasion to fructify
> the knowledge which the writing in the air of the dancer has offered.
>
> (NRCD notes)

Laban saw ballet, at its best, not as a status-laden extension of power and spectacle, but as an expression of what is humanly possible to achieve.

It is the mature performer's job to "become aware of invisible and inherent realities. The gift of the actor is to produce this telepathy. ... It [drama] is like a common prayer, but not formulated in words. Everybody works for this effect" (NRCD notes). In other words, the performer's job is to present such fullness and depth that the audience recognizes both the human story and the transcendence of the every-day in every performance.

ACCESSING THE MYSTERIOUS

Laban's mysticism merged with his passion for clarity, especially pre-verbal clarity, of communication. While much of theater relies on text, Laban's contributions are in helping performers find that part of themselves that predates language, reaching back to experiences from one's early years to find nuance and clarification of qualities.

He saw a continuum of the telling of the human story that ranged from primitive rituals to highly evolved abstract ballets, especially as the audience's active witnessing informed the work. He felt that any play was like a ballet in that it is an arrangement and guidance of the action.

> The actor needs the readiness of as many viewpoints of the audience as possible to merge into a common receptivity, because it is from this intangible but powerful stream that he receives his own power to make the spell always more convincing and irresistible. This is today, as it was in the ancient religious rituals and ceremonies, the essence of that freeing of the human spirit from the bondage of personal worries and everyday considerations, fears, and pre-occupations

(NRCD notes)

In this sense, theater as well as ballet is "irrational" (Laban's word) because the audience is partly responsible for the success of the experience. The performer in a ballet represents a person or a character "driven over the stage by a storm of willpower or emotion, like an autumnal leaf is driven over the ground by a real gale." Laban saw the embodying of a sequence of Efforts that resonate with the audience member's experiences of change and constancy and the struggle with both as the essential aim of the artist.

In that sense, every performance is a kind of hero's journey, one in which the character must truly live through the internal shifts and pulls of the context of the story or setting. One way to experience the depth of what Laban suggests is to extend and expand on the dance or staging, removing any text, and discovering the dance of emotions underneath the surface of a scene or section. Once the underlying "storm" is revealed, the performer can return to the appropriate level of telling or revealing, with all of the unpacking under the surface, but newly clarified.

"Dance is Effort training. Where dance is weak, scanty, rotten, there Effort training is weak, scanty, rotten," he wrote, thereby placing himself in the realm of the expressionists, who valued such specificity and clarity of particular qualities. "A man is not important through his symbol (his name) nor through his appearance (body-mind presence) but through his life-story (sequence of events)," he wrote in his personal notes (NRCD). These two beliefs in combination reveal the essence of Laban's philosophy and training-practice of what he called the "god-man-dancer," or the fully human performer who transcends the everyday behaviors and achieves a level of universality.

In order to achieve such universality, Effort qualities must come from deep inside the history and the understandings of the human body in motion: "All living creatures are constantly consummating their own internal rhythm," he wrote. Movement behavior is therefore both summative and formative; it is a result of experiences even as it forms those experiences.

In *The Mastery of Movement*, Laban articulated the differences between artifice and authenticity, and explained why he developed and explored the nature of what is true and essential:

> The value of characterization through dance-like mime movements lies in the avoidance of the simple imitation of external movement peculiarities. Such imitation does not penetrate to the hidden recesses of man's inner Effort. We need an authentic symbol of the inner vision to effect contact with the audience, and this contact can be achieved only if we have learned to think in terms of movement. The central problem of theater is to learn how to use this thinking for the purposes of the mastery of movement.
>
> (Laban, 1971, p. 20)

Laban did not separate applications of Effort work to business and industry from Effort work for the stage. He was, as we have seen, interested in artistry and effectiveness in all of human movement. In notes at the NRCD, he defined the broadest range of applications of Effort work:

- Business
- Labour/industrial man
- Agriculture
- International policy (Armament and disarmament included)

He went on to write that in observing the movements of people more closely one gets the impression that they are representing a kind of description of some experiences of man, which cannot be told in any other way. The possibilities for cross-cultural communication, adapting and understanding become evident and, indeed, the emerging field of peace studies recognizes the value of observing such "writing in the air."

As an example, Deborah Heifetz-Yahav, a Laban movement analyst in Israel, has analyzed the dance of interactions between Palestinian and Israeli generals in the post-Oslo Peace Accords period. The differences between the cultural patterns and Effort life are as apparent as they are heart-breaking. The analysis reveals how close the two cultures were in their yearnings for peaceful resolutions, but how their inability to adapt to each other's patterns kept them from finding common ground.

SYNTHESIS OF THE ELEMENTS

Laban's description of what good dancers are doing takes into account the interplay and synthesis of the elements of movement:

> They are dividing space and time in more or less regular segments and stretches. They accentuate more of these stretches in a curious way, using hereby certain amounts of muscular energy and these amounts of force are evolving in well-regulated sequences. They alternate between a liberal use of the flow of their energy and a more restrained use of it, and all of this seems to make more sense at least in causing to them a certain pleasure. Spectators can participate in this pleasure if the dances are well-performed, that means, if all this sequences happen in a certain comprehensible order.
>
> In what this order consists is not so easy to say. The evolutions of dancers can be very varied and still there exist movement sequences, which we would not call dances even if we use this word in a very wide sense. The movement sequences must center about some definite inner experience, they cannot change all too dramatically from one inner experience to the other.
>
> To call these inner experiences emotions would be quite right, if we content ourselves with much more general expression. If we are able to state that one dance expresses pleasure and the other sorrows and a third or fourth one perhaps fierceness or gentleness, we presuppose obviously that certain forms of this writing in the air mean really pleasure or sorrow or others fierceness or gentleness.

Some people will disregard the writing in the air which the dancer does—and so also its meaning-all together. These people will see dance in its outer purpose, social intercourse, flirtation, and nothing else. Others may have heard that dance is with primitive or exotic people sometimes a part of religious worship, and they take it then as a kind of performance, in which like with the dancing dervishes something like the "dance of the stars round god" is represented.

The student of movement will have a quite different vision. It looks to him almost as if the dancers would have some intuitive knowledge about a lot of things, after which modern science is striving. Some dancers are full of revelations for the anatomist and physiologist, the student of the structure and function of the living body and especially of course of the human body. This is not only the case with acrobatic dancers in which a wonderful display of exact muscle functions is given; expressive dances also can reveal a lot about the inner structure and function especially about nerve reactions.

(NRCD notes)

In the end, Laban was left with questions: How does the dancer recapitulate the inner structures and functions so well? Is dance a way of knowing; an awareness of the ancient patterns as they inform new comprehension? The approach he began to define in *The Mastery of Movement* is only the beginning of a process of answering those questions.

People are inspired by the penetration into the world of silence, of the possibility that both dance and acting (or performance art) allows. To see something created from nothing but the material of the human body and mind/imagination is better, in Laban's sensibility, than a "crude imitation of reality."

Laban believed, rightly or wrongly, that he was at the gateway of a new form of acting; one that honored the approaches of the past, but that incorporated new ways of experimentation and awareness of human growth and psyche. His approach was, and is, an entry into performance that is at once authentic, embodied, empathetic and educated.

NOTATION AND OBSERVATION

The notation system was developed by others; Laban, as stated in Part I, lost some interest when the symbology became reflective of static points in space, as opposed to dynamical shifts. However, he came back to the system as a result of his work with F. C. Lawrence on Effort. Capturing Effort changes in notation appealed to his desire to capture the essence of movement as shifts in attitudes and inclinations. Laban saw the use of notation for performing artists as a way of encapsulating historically and psychologically significant ways of moving; not only as a way of preserving, but also of accessing a range of choices.

In the dance training he developed, capturing Effort changes through notation is a way of developing the eye to see and commit to specificities of quality. The actor/dancer/performer can "read" movement and recapitulate the ephemeral aspects.

The microanalysis of movement that Laban's notation reveals allows for specificity as well as potency. He saw it as a way of looking into the movement more deeply and less imitatively. The observation process itself yields evidence-based creativity.

The process he articulated is as follows:

1   observe systematically and procedurally
2   start at the beginning—what is the first "event"? The "entrance"?
3   Note how the person enters, walks, stops
4   Note latent capacities as well as what appear to be typical tendencies
5   One's own movement makeup is the ground on which to build; "Know thyself"

(Laban, 1971, p. 98)

This last recommendation is, to an extent, what sets the Laban work apart from other systematic approaches to analysis and character-building through movement. The human body is notoriously self-referential; as Sam Thornton said, quoted in Part I (page 37): "We all live in the same world, but we don't all see the same world." It is only through owning one's biases that one can build upon them, augment and generate new ways of behaving. Therefore, unlike movement approaches that take performers to generic neutrality, the Laban work builds upon the liveliness and predilections already present.

Neutrality, in Laban's approach, is unattainable, and perhaps, undesirable as well. Characters are never neutral, and Laban believed that through Effort training, such exercises directed at achieving neutrality or a blank slate of body would be unnecessary. The body already has character, and pattern, and the personal style of a mover must be known, explored and built upon.

At the center of the work, therefore, there is no vacancy or undifferentiated flow, but tension. Laban wrote about tension as the waxing and waning of movement preferences and attitude changes, of the pulls each individual feels into space, towards or away from objects. He differentiated "pompous gesticulations, melodramatic sentimentality, dance like overacting" from "naturalism devoid of any expression at all, imitation of the everyday life and passivity" and found both approaches wanting. He valued "the almost invisible finer movement tensions between people conversing." Inner tension, outwardly expressed makes the performance alive and real.

As an experiment, if one moves one hand forward in space, as a gesture, but the movement has no tension at all, no drama, nothing is revealed except direction and rate of movement. Add a countering tension from the stomach, or the heart, and meaningfulness appears.

In order to master these tensions, one must actually practice and embody the widest possible range of choices. Therefore, practicing specific patterns over and over again, as well as observing and embodying unfamiliar or uncomfortable patterns, is key to the process of building up the performer's toolkit. Laban cautioned against overly conscious or precious analysis however. He described the best process as keying into the essential underpinnings of movement, and most importantly, as a synthesis of scientific and artistic observation.

In notes he wrote around the time of *The Mastery of Movement*, Laban said: "Few people will realize that a page of musical notes is to a great extent a description or prescription of bodily motivations or of the way how to move your muscles, limbs, breathing organs ... in order to produce certain effects" (NRCD notes). In his mind, the notation system was also a way into the layers and richness of movement; not a reductionist exercise in writing, but a potent method of understanding the essential layers of any movement event or phrase. To paraphrase further, the power is not given in the single letters or signs of the notation, but in the grouping the arrangements provide.

THE STAGE AS LABORATORY

The theater, he wrote, is where we go to see life "in contemplations and through a magnifying glass" (1971, p. 107). To Laban, a person who has no interest in man's strivings is hardly an actor, nor is he yet a human being. He described the connection between what happens on the stage and what human beings learn from engaging with performance as personal responsibility, what they come to understand about consequences of actions; and as a civilizing process.

Action and interaction are the baseline of learning about the world; in that sense, man creates his own fate. The constant renegotiation of inner and outer behaviors yields both character and values. Individual motivations vary greatly, and therefore, as interactions unfurl onstage, greater range and complexity of character and situation can be revealed.

Ageless struggles are the fodder of great drama and ballet, and Laban saw the Effort work (space-weight-time-flow in combinations that reveal intent and attitude) as the tapestry threads of human interactions, both dramatic and comedic.

> All Effort action or reaction is an approach towards values, the primary value being the maintenance or achievement of the balance needed for the individual's survival ... the actor is the mediator between the solitary self of the spectator and the world of values.
>
> (Laban, 1971, pp. 119–21)

Therefore, performers need to practice extremes and the in-between; to have access to the essence and the complexity of many human behaviors. People do not stay in one pattern or one attitude. During the shifts some elements change, some remain and persist, others disappear. Humans manifest disharmonies and create dramatic tensions, and these are observable, replicable and revealing of deeper layers of the psyche.

An experiment from theater to understand how Effort plays out might be to take a scene—for example, the handkerchief scene from *Othello*—and remove the dialogue, but think the dialogue as the actors move around the room. The qualities of the glances, the juxtapositions, the pauses, and the unfolding of the story itself can reveal much about the layers of intrigue, love and betrayal that Shakespeare was writing about.

Laban's basic understanding of theory-into-practice was best stated by himself:

> Man's material body is like an anvil on which the blows of life incessantly
> beat ... The power to make people believe in such almost ineffable things
> resides entirely in the artist's well-cultivated movement capacity.
>
> (Laban, 1971, pp. 158–60)

In additional notes from the NRCD, he pointed out that "any activity
is a sequence of Efforts—partly visible in rhythms of body movements
or somatic indications of dynamics, partly audible in words." He wrote
further about the "rhythms of ideas", including metaphoric expressions that are used in imagistic or symbolic sequences.

Laban directly addressed the Cartesian mind–body split in *The
Mastery of Movement*. He believed and promoted the idea that somatic
and mental Efforts are combined into action sequences in which the
flow is characterized by changes (the appearance and disappearance of
phenomena) in the flow of the action. Some of these qualities serve
the action; others are ancillary and idiosyncratic. Laban also understood that the ancillary and idiosyncratic qualities are the most
revealing of personal style and character.

THERAPY

Effort study yields more than improvement of performance. Laban
also understood that Effort practice reveals internal conflicts and
struggles with the ego. For example, one can observe particular dis-
crepancies between the postural qualities and the gestural qualities in
some psychiatric disorders. Through the process of attuning to the
underlying or latent qualities, a client or patient can be supported into
and through a course of healing and reclaiming of the self. Laban
himself worked with people in this way, most notably described by
Mary Wigman. He was engaged by an extremely elderly woman to
teach her to dance again. The woman was wheelchair-bound, but
through his support and attunement to her, Laban managed to get her
to stand and sway, and, ultimately, to dance with him.

In this sense, he was an early dance therapist, intuiting the possibility of intervention and developmental treatment. In fact, he understood development to be a process of selection via the elimination and
acquisition of Efforts, a theoretical approach to therapy that was later
developed further by Dr Judith Kestenberg, a child psychiatrist who
developed the Kestenberg Movement Profile.

Laban noted that the tendency to consciously and conspicuously change qualities, to conceal and reveal Efforts, and to freeze expression in patterned and predictable ways is how humans identify and recognize the individual. He wrote in his notes that voluntary dissolution or masking of Efforts could be seen as a form of deception, whereas involuntary dissolution or masking of Efforts could be seen as states of dysfunction or illness. The attempt to mask is visible, just as the attempt to perform is seen as just that: an attempt. But it is also possible to see the struggle of an individual to drop a mask and to be freed from dysfunctional patterns as a struggle to heal.

Taking further the theory of how Effort reveals personality and the conflicts therein, he added that any living movement has the possibility of a countermove in itself. The countermovement might be something like falling backwards when one intends to move forwards, or dropping into passivity at a moment when direct action is required. Effort preferences can lead the body into having internal "arguments" about where one is heading. In such instances, one can literally find oneself coming and going, stumbling, tripping, or displaying a lack of commitment to any one direction. But when such counter moves are not restricted or confused they can also function as counter-flow, counter-space, counter-weightedness, or counter tension.

Countering is different from conflict in that give-and-take is inherently present; countering is, literally, the dance of negotiation. In inner conflict, the mind bounces from one pull to the other, and reconciliation between the two is often the challenge of the dramatic, onstage and in real life. In countering, the fullness of choices is palpable, and the tensions between them serve to enhance awareness of the degree of personal agency the mover has.

An exercise to illustrate this: Try walking forward, while imagining being called from behind, noting the negotiation that takes place internally in order to respond to both aims. Which direction wins out?

We have understood that Laban favored movement over position, dynamism over stasis. "Life is a special rhythmical case," he wrote. "Existence as a polarized unit is not life. Life is full of organic radiation." (NRCD notes) The study of Effort provides a way for living beings to become more conscious and integrated with biophysical realities and to utilize these for creative and healing purposes. He wrote that "we must distinguish between the psychology of thought and the psychology of adaptive acts. But in the end, there is no other

function than physicality." Our behaviors and their patterns
we are conscious of as well as what we are not conscio
through movement, the unconscious can be made visible, and recovered
as part of the fabric of the self.

GRAPHING LIFE

Laban loved visual representations of ephemeral ideas. He made lots of
charts, many of which found their way into his books in narrative
forms. The one that follows is from random notes, but further
explains his notion of life as movement:

MASS:
   Accumulation = tension
   Disaccumulation = Relaxation

ENERGY:
   Accumulation = Charge
   Disaccumulation = Discharge

The rhythmical accumulation of both mass and energy is life, which
yields change and ongoingness. Experiment with how the words above
affect any gesture. Tension and Charge are words that would inspire
Bound Flow, whereas Relaxation and Discharge yield Free Flow. Laban
saw Bound Flow as controlled successive discharge and Free Flow as
spontaneous eruptive discharge. He preferred derivations of Bound
Flow for performer training, in part because he believed Bound Flow
has more "charge," which yields richer characters.

EXERTION AND RECUPERATION

Another graph:

Relaxation	Tension
Discharge	Charge

Relaxation and Discharge in combination would appear to be close to
what Laban later called the indulging side of Effort, or "going with" a

quality while Charge and Tension in combination would be the condensing side, or fighting against a quality. He did not believe in the positive or negative aspects of either condensing or indulging; he knew that it is the changing movement that informs and communicates and not the particular content of that changing movement. He did believe that actors and dancers could use more training and experience with the Tension/Charge side of the graph, but then, he never encountered the twenty-first century educational system, nor the instant gratification world of rewards and consequences in twenty-first century business, where, all too often, a little Free Flow/Discharge would be welcome!

Laban wrote that Effort facilitates and regulates choices of recreational activity in that the individual will often seek out recuperative ways of balancing the requirements of one's work with sports that require other ways of expressing one's self. In his day, such activities might include competitive sports situations such as tennis or golf, or walking in the country, or swimming. Each of these has aspects of condensing (tension and charge) as well as indulging (relaxation and discharge). Such would be appropriate balances to the workday, which would have required both ends of the spectrum as well. As The Mastery of Movement (Laban Movement Analysis) is used nowadays, Effort analysis of one's workday often reveals a high degree of imbalance, with an excessive amount of tension and charge, requiring deep meditative release as recuperation. All too often also, tension and discharge are paired, in the direction of co-workers or management, as explosive tantrums, and relaxation and charge are paired, in the direction of hardcore competitive sports.

The goal towards a healthier balance would be to foster a fuller range of behaviors throughout the day, including tensions appropriate to tasks, with deep breaths and release as needed, recharging throughout and discharging appropriately, preferably accompanied by a sense of humor.

SCRIPTS AND APPLICATIONS TO THEATER

Laban proposed a number of scenes and ideas for performance works; none of which were ever produced. While he was living at the school in Addlestone, Surrey, teaching rarely, but providing an immense presence, he toyed with recreating some of his earlier tanztheater pieces.

When he was at Dartington and afterwards, he spoke with Michael Chekhov and the actor Basil Langton about ways to approach theater training using his theories and practices and his work was advanced in such training by Geraldine Stephenson and Yat Malmgren. It is impossible to know if anyone picked up and ran with any of his script ideas, but they are useful as demonstrations of ways to explore the application of theory to practice:

> Scenes and Ideas for Dramatic Group Improvisations:
> War-drama (with strong psychological and religious background)
> Protestant against Catholic (Henry VIII)
> Family reunion
> (Laban went on to do a kind of storyboard, using Effort and space-maps, along with production notes).
>
> (NRCD notes)

THREE MIME PLAYS

In *The Mastery of Movement*, Laban provided ideas for three scenarios that can be developed as classroom exercises or movement scripts. The first is a version of the beginning of the story in Mozart's opera *The Magic Flute*. He called it "Tamino's Quest" and it is a story of the boy-into-man journey in which unrequited love is a driving force. Laban was fascinated with Mozart's tale, and in Chapter 3 of this book (p. 75) we saw how significant the "Queen of the Night" archetype was to him. In the description in *The Mastery of Movement* of the characters and their movement qualities, she is foiled by the young man, who sees through her disguises.

The second mime-play Laban proposes is based on the *Dance of the Seven Veils* of Salome. A dialogue between the head of John the Baptist, who speaks to Salome while she dances and the silent dancing Salome, the piece is about an older man's lust for a young woman and the layers of betrayal and yearning she arouses in him. Through his imploring accusations, Salome finds her sexual power in the movement, and thus her political power.

The third scenario is that of the "Golden Shawl", a story of transcendence and redemption in a fishing village. A young girl is given a golden shawl, which causes her to emerge from shyness into full bloom and that causes the village to become contentious and to fight among themselves over such a gift. Those who behave with violence and impulsivity are injured and thought dead until the redemptive powers of love and forgiveness that the golden shawl represents appear. Laban provided a description that included the groupings of performers and movement qualities juxtaposed against the actions going on in the scene. He pointed out that he could give great detail in how such a story ought to be told, but that instead he provides an outline, with suggestions for particular choreography and attitudes to be expressed. It is a kind of storyboard with added color.

All of the scenarios, including the ones he made notes on but did not develop, contain themes of subversion, sexual awakenings or conflicts resolved. The characters are human and they have much to express and to overcome.

THEATER IS LIFE

In another set of handwritten notes, Laban asked: "Which are the elements of theatrical art?"

He answered himself:

> That the essence of mime is the gift and the art to express thoughts feelings and volitions though bodily movements. The producer and even the poet are the instruments of the strange force of mime which gets hold of the actor, the carrier of the waves of movement. These artists are results and not elements.
>
> (NRCD notes)

The theater, to Laban, is a place for audience response, but all changes and is changed.

> No tribe, no peoples, no civilisations exist in which mime is entirely lacking. The healthy drive of human nature to express its emotions through bodily motion can be repressed in times of inner stagnation. The unwavering wave of expressive movement gliding through humanity is in some periods more magical, in others more ecstatic. Abstract pieces of pure movement expression alternate with more concrete representations of the struggles of man. Yet, they are one thing, one great stream of formative energy which does not start or end with men or the life organisms.
>
> Artificial mime, the intended performance of tensions, feelings, of connections of happenings is never seen in real life. This artificial approach is play

and not work. The urge to play is a primary drive of man. Yet play is a useful thing, as any other manifestation of nature. Play is the basis of our lifelong education. Play is a means of inner and outer recreation and regeneration, and it is in playing with our dreams of highest ideals that we discover the Beyond. Play is the ground on which the greatest gift of man—imagination—grows. Play gives us the awareness of our capacities and possibilities.

(NRCD notes)

Play, therefore, including experimentation, is the stuff from which the human spirit makes art. The dancer, the actor, the mime, all engage with the process of research and innovation, investigation and play, in the service of imagination. What a sad and empty place the world would be without it.

MOVEMENT IS LIVING

In *The Mastery of Movement*, Laban returned to the Asconan ideal of Love-Work-Play, with a renewed understanding of how the three reinforce and inform each other. It is safe to say that the essence of his theory and all he has left us is simply about the triangle of integrated life.

In notes that might have been meant for a poem, he wrote:

our movements are imperfect crystallizations, fragments of directional tensions, diluted into the mortality of our time-feelings. Space appears as more of a body, but within a set of rays and lightening strokes in single moments of

magical or
ecstatical

transfigurations.
It is a play with concrete conjurer-tricks to dance. We get out of reality and bring the spectator out of his blunt belief in a minor reality of everyday worries. The greater reality of united space penetrates our body our limbs and makes them

float and wave
flutter and glide

piercing into depths where words alone cannot reach, pressing knotting our attention and paralysing our intentions
pulling, lifting our shape to a dissolution of all former binding

untying our fetters

This is the might of movement, of play, of mime!

(NRCD notes)

Thus Laban shares his perspectives on the role of theater performance in the lives of human beings, and thus he prescribes the ways in which performers can master the art of being fully human. With stories at the heart of every performance, the goal was to help people find their way to the essence and truth of those stories we tell ourselves over and over, hoping to learn anew. As he summarized:

> Events ... as well as movements, have to be carefully selected and composed into a whole, if an effective work of stagecraft is to be built up ... Then and only then is it possible, with the help of the play and the movements of which the performance consists, to paint in the spectator's heart a seed from which a flower of the inner garden may grow. It may even happen that fruit will succeed the flower; fruit that takes the form of a new attitude towards life. The power to make people believe in such ineffable things resides entirely in the artist's well-cultivated movement capacity.

> (Laban, 1971, p. 160)

The Mastery of Movement does not contain all of the approaches currently used in practice, but it is the bedrock of the values and ideals of contemporary movement theater work, especially as those ideals are applied to performance, leadership, discourse analysis and therapy. It holds seeds of wisdom and insight, which Laban's students carried forward into new applications.

As in all of his work, the goal is freedom and access to a range of authentic expressions. He addressed the artist in each of us, urging us to find our true centers and our fullest range.

3

THE TANZTHEATER AND ANALYSIS OF A WORK

Die Grünen Clowns

At the beginning of the 1920s, the training programs Laban had devised for students all over Europe, including the emerging notation system, the freie tanz, the movement choirs, and the rest of the curriculum did not yet contain a study of choreosophy (the aesthetics of movement), choreography (which he thought of as the notation of movement) or choreology (the analysis of movement for the purpose of making dances). The rise of the tanztheater throughout the 1920s clarified the need for more organized and specific training, however. The schools and the curriculum within them had to address a more systematic approach to training as well as a more divergent approach to the creative process.

The tanztheater, which required specificity of expression, clarity of technique and rampant innovation, provided a laboratory for experimentation in a variety of creative approaches to art making. In this section of the book, we will discover how all of those threads unfolded into one of his works: *Die Grünen Clowns* (*The Green Clowns*).

TANZTHEATER PRIVILEGED DANCE OVER MUSIC AND VISUAL COMPONENTS

In the early to mid-1920s, the tanztheater galvanized the European performance world. Because Laban and Wigman placed movement over music, costume and all external theatrical devices, and through the refinement of physically expressive and spatially clear storytelling, the dance itself became the primary medium. And although music, costume and all external devices were often present and supported the movement, the unfolding of the story happened through the medium of dance.

Laban's approach was in contrast to the music-centric theories and practices of Dalcroze's Eurhythmics work and moved beyond the unrestrained, free flowing movement that Isadora Duncan performed to Chopin and Beethoven. He was after something more specific and discursive. Whereas Duncan's movement was expressive in a general way, she also believed she was channeling the music and the classicism of the ancient Greeks. Dalcroze taught movement as the externalization of the form and expressivity of the movement. But Laban was interested in the movement moment itself, its content, meaning and relationship to the human spirit. He was not concerned with the embodiment of music or a particular aesthetic ideal; he preferred specific and potent movement that was expressive and detailed.

Laban wrote in "Das Tanztheater" in the journal *Licht luft Leben Verlag Die Schonheit* (*The Journal of Aesthetics and Beauty*) (Dresden, 1924, Vol. XXII) that tanztheater was a new form of art. In this new genre, the movement itself was the main concern; everything else was secondary. Music could be simple or simply not necessary. Music could even be just noises, or the sound of breathing. The same went for costumes: he used whatever he found or felt might work.

As in all of his writing throughout his life, Laban crossed into the poetic realms, waxing rhapsodically about the art form in "Das Tanztheater": "Dance transports, like a poem or drama. It can be witty; can be humorous, rich and colorful. It's different from music" (Laban, 1924). Laban wrote that there was, for him, a greater degree of relationship between dance and poetry and dance and mimetic drama than there was with music, despite his ongoing comparisons. He understood that dance is not easily put into words and that is why people relate it to music or acting; but in the end, it stands only for itself. He described dance as the Ur-kunst, the Ur-art, or the primary and earliest form of art. Music and drama, he wrote, came later and used elements of dance.

"This new dance theater aims for finding a synthesis of all possibilities of expression and bringing those together again. This synthesis can be dance tragedy, dance ballad (song), dance comedy, or a move-ment symphony" (Laban, 1924).

Despite his stated belief that dance is less related to music than it is to poetry, analogies to musical form and theory abound in his writing.

> Dance has things to say and express that cannot be said through music or acting, and in a deep way. It is the music of the limbs. The logic of the dance movement has to be harmonic in order to let the dance event be a symbol for a life event that makes us happy or sad, but that touches us.
>
> (Laban, 1924, *Licht luft Leben Verlag Die Schonheit*, Dresden, Vol. XXII, translated by Sabine Fichter)

He also questioned how far abstraction could go and decided that good art must maintain a close relationship to life itself. Dance is integral to being alive, to being human. And yet, dance is, in a way, an abstraction. It's both inherent to humanity and a way to be more human. For example, Laban understood the use of masks in dance as both a reflection as well as an extension of human personality. In that sense, dance is a kind of mask that reveals as much as it extends the face of the individual.

TANZTHEATER DROVE THE NEED FOR AN ANALYSIS AND NOTATION SYSTEM

One of Laban's main concerns was that dance had not yet defined its own language. He made an analogy to the other art forms: music and drama, both of which have conventions, theory, and a textual form. In so doing, he made a case for his notation system, but more than that, he was emancipating dance, at least in his mind, from the other art forms, and providing a means whereby dance could be preserved and recaptured as movement, and therefore maintain value.

Other notation systems existed, and dance had a vocabulary of steps from ballet. But the new dance, freed from those conventions and patterns, required a different way of thinking about how to capture and archive what was essentially ephemeral and inventive.

In developing the notation system, Laban freed dance and captured it again, but he captured it as an ever-changing, context-influenced phenomenon. One can make decisions and do so within a range of choices inherent in the notation system, through an interpretative and synthesizing process. The categories of Body, Space and Effort co-exist, inform each other, and transcend the limits of thinking in terms of steps or floor patterns, musical contexts or theatrical terms.

He began to equate movement sequences that occupied the areas of space above the waist as "high dances", equivalent to the songs of the soprano, and dances close to the earth as "low dances", like the songs of the baritone. His comparison of the soprano and the baritone goes beyond the amplitude of the vocal ranges of both. He saw the relationship between space and style as a justification for men performing, (an issue he appeared to be deeply concerned about) because, he said, in art, all options have to be present and available and true to life. Just as opera requires the presence of the baritone, men have to be onstage, fulfilling their roles. Such roles and the predilections of men and women differ. Each type of physicality requires different dynamic support.

In an article on anatomy in the journal *Licht luft Leben Verlag Die Schonheit* (1924), he wrote about the technique and body training he was beginning to develop. He used the words rising and sinking, descriptors of full body movement that are still used to clarify a particular way of going up and down in space. He wrote about tension and recuperation from tension. He pointed out that the body can widen and narrow, mainly through breathing. For a tiny second, there is a point of rest in breathing, and that moment organizes the one that follows. If a mover wanted to pick up something heavy from the floor, he/she could do this with both quickness and lightness, and then use strong and sustained qualities, which produce complex phrases of meaningful expression. He wrote about movement phrases and that these are not even and unchanging. He believed that the body organizes movement into both evocative and utilitarian segments of differing lengths and emphases.

Imagine playing a character, such as a clown, who enters a space, looks around to take in all of it with a light, quick inhalation that causes a step backwards, with a narrowing of the body shape. Then the character takes a lingering step forwards, reaches down to pick up an object, grabs it, looks at it quickly and then tosses it to the side, turning the head away at the same moment.

Now imagine the exact same sequence as performed by a character such as a heroic knight. Meaning changes with the changing context of the character, but it is still recognizable as meaningful and communicative human movement. Laban's analysis of movement into Body, Effort and Space allows for replicability without the loss of choice and human creativity.

Dancers also must learn to change between stability and mobility, widening and narrowing, expanding and contracting (which he sees as a more general growing and shrinking than widening and narrowing), etc. This exploration of opposites, he wrote, is the origin of beautiful contrasts and all beauty is based on that harmonic change. "This gives a healthy order and structure to our life. And learning about these movement laws, man will be a master of his environment and the dancer will be a master of his space" (Laban, 1926). (See the concept of "mastery" in Part II.)

In his 1920 book, *Die Welt des Tanzers*, Laban began to parse the aspects of movement that comprise dance: rhythm (time), space and what he called tensions. He did not see rhythm, for example, as being merely a series of movements proceeding in time, with accents or forces. He understood rhythm to be multidimensional and meaningful. The degree to which movement has force and fluency, tension and release matters to the audience's understanding of the layers of meaning in the dance.

As he further explained in *Choreographie* (1926): The explanation of the world of dance forms must not be confined to an enumeration of rigid states. This world must be considered as undulations (wavings, transformation) alive with constant change" (quoted in Bartenieff *et al.*, 1970, p. 5).

Thus and despite his early enamoration of tableaus vivants, Laban found that the essence of meaning in dance came not from positions or poses, but from evolving and unfolding changes towards and away from points in space and in response to internal and external phenomena.

The period 1928–32 brought another level of development for the notation that Laban was developing with Albrecht Knust and the other dancers. The journal *Schrifftanz* debuted following Laban's presentation of the new notation system at the Second Dancer's Congress, at Essen. The editor, Alfred Schlee, was a young music publisher. At the beginning, the magazine was to be devoted strictly to Labanotation and there were to be four editions per year. The narrow focus was not practical, however, and so the writing expanded to include all types of writing about dance: historical, critical and theoretical analyses.

Schrifftanz was by all accounts a beautifully executed artifact, with covers by Picasso and Schlemmer and an advisory board consisting of luminaries such as Fritz Böhme, the historian, Hans Brandenberg, the critic and writer, Oskar Schlemmer, and Bronislava Nijinska. Notators from all over Europe and the United States were listed, demonstrating that notation was a growing field beyond the borders of Germany.

In 1929, the tanztheater was represented in the journal by articles about Wigman and Schlemmer, Dussia Bereska in Northern Italy, Harold Kreutzberg and Yvonne Georgi touring the United States, and an announcement of a public meeting with both Laban and Wigman to discuss plans for a State College for Dance, an idea that never came to fruition.

In the January 1929 issue, a section of a small dance piece was notated. The piece was entitled *Die Grünen Clowns* (*The Green Clowns*). The score was from a section entitled "Zeitlupe" (Slow Motion). Dussia Bereska is listed as the choreographer for that section, but the overall work was a Laban creation.

Laban wrote about why the notation was so important to dance at this time:

> Kinetography or movement notation has two objectives, which need to be clearly distinguished.
>
> The first objective is the capturing of movement sequences and dances. The advantages of such a possibility are easy to see; they have been recognized for centuries and have been continually sought, through experiments with varying degrees of success.
>
> The other objective is, from a conceptual point of view, far the more important. It deals with defining the movement process through analysis and thus freeing it from the kind of vagueness which has made the language of dance appear unclear and monotonous.
>
> (From 1928, "Basic Principles of Movement Notation", *Schrifftanz*, Vol. I, No. 1, July, p. 32)

TANZTHEATER INSPIRED NEW CONTEXTS AND FORM

Laban continued to develop his own exploration of tensions: spatial, relational, social and expressive. Evelyn Dörr describes Laban's work in and around 1928 as a radicalization of the expressionist foundation, drawn out through abstracting tensions inherent in crystalline forms (2003, *Dance Chronicle* article, pp. 1–29). Laban's drawings from this time reflect his understanding of the underlying laws of gravity and form, as well as his aesthetic of interrupting form with something that is human and idiosyncratic. To him, the tension between human and the natural laws is the stuff of art.

How far did Laban feel abstraction could go? Only as far as the movement keeps a close relationship to "life itself," he wrote. "It's in the nature of the dance that there is a necessity to the relationship to being alive, to humanity" (Laban, 1924).

He was fascinated with the spectrum of the familiar to the novel, and part of the tension he describes over and over again in his tanztheater writings explores the familiar body-based expressions (gestures) in relation to ever-evolving abstractions of spatial pulls and crystalline forms. Dörr quotes Laban from the 1926 book *Choreographie*: "he describes how a form 'is then dissolved, the process through which it passes into related forms', eventually via related forms reaching less familiar ones" (Dörr, 2003, p. 8).

In *The Green Clowns*, such everyday gestures that extend into the grotesque or novel are both recognizable and tickle the imagination. When a clown drapes herself over another clown, the movement is reminiscent of the human need to reach out for what we need (in this case, support) and to over state and overreach such needs to the point of absurdity. The draping is repeated throughout one section of the work, as both a comment on and a reflection of a tendency to exaggerate and embellish. The movement is carried into abstraction and evolution, but the meaning is not lost, but rather, universalized.

TANZTHEATER BALANCED THE ABSTRACT AND THE LITERAL

Laban's approach was not simply to abstract movement from mime or story; he wanted to be sure that the dance always had a relationship to human experiences, feelings, and behaviors. But he also believed dance was inherently an abstraction. Therefore his realm was metaphor, not literality. The specificity and detail in the movement were imagistic and referential, symbolic and often ironic, but also simple and clear.

A simple wave of the hand, as in a gesture of greeting, serves as an example of the dichotomy reconnected. Such a gesture can be performed in many different ways; all refer to the same message of greeting, but one can convey a multitude of nuanced communiqués by clarifying and specifying the details within the wave. An example is the beauty-queen greeting, as she is carried through the streets in a parade, sitting atop a convertible. The direct but general gaze, the even phrasing as the hand turns slightly from side to side, palm revealed to the crowd like a lighthouse beacon, all performed with an unchanging smile, conveys something different from the politician's leap onto a platform with a raised arm that pumps as she waves the entire hand quickly. Both are greetings, but each is specific to the context and to the purpose of the performance.

In *Die Welt des Tanzers* (1920) Laban wrote: "Dance is gesture, i.e. a synthesis of body tension, emotional excitation, and imagining" (Bartenieff *et al.*, 1970, p. 6). Whereas the theorists Dalcroze and Delsarte linked meaning in movement to meaning in other modalities—music and spoken word—and early modern dancers found meaning in cultural references, simple beauty and their own gesture life, Laban tried to unpack meaning from pure elements, as an anthropologist reconstructs meaning directly from artifacts. But as an archeologist of sorts, Laban was also interested in the deeper, human story buried within the movement. And he valued the movement intrinsically, as a manifestation of human spirit or soul. In the examples above, of the beauty queen and the politician, what drives each to the roles they play is something profoundly felt: an identification with a particular way of being in the world that goes deeper than performing a task or communicating a message. Gestures, therefore, can be both universal communications of message as well as specific to identity, role, and culture. Dancers must understand both aspects.

In *Die Welt des Tanzers*, Laban described the process of coming into the profound world of a dancer:

> We hardly see with our eyes, any more than we hear with our ears. To concentrate on the eye: An agglomeration which has arisen from the specially formed harmonic form of uniform infinity is clearly and roughly mirrored by one of our organs, the eye. Clearly in the sense of being explicable, our experience interprets this as a space-claiming agglomeration, a thing. Our research interprets the eye as a darkroom. The process of being and recognizing the nature

of the object seen is naturally not explained by this. What sees? The eye? The whole being? … One evening I go into the woods. Tree branches rise and fall around a patch of empty sky. A strip of clouds passes steeply and obliquely across this patch. Below it, next to it is a star. I am stirred, moved.

The path leads me to a place where an agglomerate chord, a tension, a thought of god awakes which has always existed but lain dormant within me. I can recall the mathematic aesthetic proportions of the phenomenon; I can be jubilant or tearful according to its effect. I can say to myself, "Tomorrow the weather will be fine." All the same, a thought of god has awoken within me. If I experience this tension fully and if I know how to weave it into my life, then I am dancer.

(Laban, 1920, Schröder translation)

The connection of what Laban called "the god within" to deeply felt and detailed expression is recognizable to anyone who practices daily in order to refine performance. To Laban, the execution of each moment was as important as the large ideas behind the pieces he developed. The training for such performances required mastery of body, mind, and soul. In Part II, we saw how the training happened, through effort study, spatial analysis and practice, and refinement of skills within the context of story and other meaning-making human experiences. Anyone who danced with him had to experience the tensions fully, and to weave it into and out of his/her own life.

TANZTHEATER PRODUCED A NEW TYPE OF CHOREOGRAPHER

In addition to his emerging theories about the categories and characteristics of movement specificity, Laban also had an evolving idea about a new type of "dancing master." Unlike the socially ascendant and advancing of political status effects of the court-based dancing masters' approach to dance training, or the dictatorial and hierarchical attitudes of the ballet masters of the nineteenth century, he preferred the notion of an independent dance director who would support the creative spirit and the deep mastery of technique in each dancer.

Beyond the individual dancer, however, he also understood that the dance director must first and foremost attend to whatever layers of meaning were necessary to serve the larger themes. The dance, he felt, consists of the individual bodies in movement as well as the spirit of the whole piece. A good director attends to both.

Laban was both a generous and an exacting man; he could be encouraging and a little brutal. For him the dance and the often-abstract stories the bodies told through movement were as important as the means whereby those stories were being told. Therefore the training his dancers underwent in the 1920s, in Germany looked nothing like the ballet classes from the days of the opera's ascendance; nor did they look like the classes at Denishawn or the Martha Graham School, later on. Laban's training was based on both exploration and refinement of the moment, which was a process of creative and divergent investigations along with feedback and discussion about the specificity and clarity of a moment.

As noted in the biographical section, classically trained ballet dancers did not take to his approach easily. His movement process was a great leveler, encouraging depth of feeling rather than virtuosity of execution, and favoring the ensemble over the star system. Daily classes in eukinetics (expression) and choreutics (space harmony, scales, theory and practice together) were taught by Laban and his assistants and experimentation with ideas was encouraged as work was created.

His main assistant in the Tanzbühne classes and performance group was Dussia Bereska, who was also his mistress and the mother of his ninth child (Little Dussia). Bereska was a Russian dancer, trained, and tempestuous by all accounts. Films from the 1920s show a beautiful and clearly expressive dancer, one who was a solo artist by temperament and talent. She could hold the stage with the tiniest of movements; she was so clear. Other dancers may have been better at the large sweeping movements, but Bereska had an elegance that was unique. She was also Laban's partner in running the company. She directed the Kammertanzbühne, or chamber groups, coaching and refining the performances.

Films from the 1920s show her to be specific and clear in her phrasing, and a deeply emotional mover. In *Orchidée* (a short film fragment from the Laban archives at Creekside), for example, a solo in which she sat cross-legged on a platform, nude from the waist up, her arms undulating with a clear connection to her entire torso; movement from the heart and soul. The piece was part of the fascination with "Orientalism" (as Ruth St. Denis also found inspiration), but the piece had a ring of authenticity: the fullness of the undulations and the clarity of expression recalls that Laban had actually spent time studying Dervish dances and had had a Sufi teacher as a boy. Possibly Bereska herself had also been directly exposed to Asian dance, as she was Russian.

Bereska also helped to develop the dance technique and curriculum
for both the movement choir and the chamber groups. Building on
what Laban and Wigman had begun to create and articulate in
Stuttgart, she made the specific refinements for clarity in space and
quality into the underpinnings of expressionist dance technique. Her
role in the development of the creation and execution of all of the
tanztheater works in the early to mid-1920s was significant, especially
as a coach for detailed expressive movement.

Laban therefore was a new kind of dance director, one who noted
the individual talents of his performers, and who encouraged and
empowered others to be part and parcel of the development of the
work, both as theory and as practice.

TANZTHEATER SHOULD NOT BE ABUSED!

Laban wrote, in 1924, that the art form of dance ought not to be
abused anymore, a lament he was to repeat to some extent for dec-
ades. He saw much to complain about with how dance was treated as
an art form by the public, but he saved some of his concern for the
creators of the art form. Bad dance theater, he stated, is the mime-
dramatic copy of life that works with conventional gestures instead of
working with space harmony, or schwingen, as he called the various
scales he was deriving at this time. When dancers simply copy

rhythmical arabesques and stereotypic exercises, they are missing the aliveness of dance. The dance should not only be controlled by the brain or intellect. One who is a "dance poet" should use the inspiration of those means of expression that are appropriate to convey the specifics of what one intended.

In support of the ideals of Ausdrucktanz (expressive dance), the films that still exist of his dance works reveal that, although the movement looks "old-fashioned" in the sense that the vocabulary contains some phrases that have become clichés, it was executed with detailed clarity. The jumpy film of Bereska performing *Orchidée* (1923) reveal characteristic (for the times) "Oriental" movement phrases, but also show her innate sense of liveliness in the midst of clear spatial configurations.

Laban saw the need for theater spaces devoted to the enhancement of the audience's perception of tanztheater works. But Laban did not have the type of large dance theater to work in (although he was often seen designing such a large space) that he thought was necessary to convey some of his larger, more myth-based works. He did feel that chamber dance, rightly done, could also convey big ideas, however. The solo dancer or small ensemble can be as compelling and moving as a song sung clearly, a sonata, an anecdote, an *aperçu*.

But for such work, Laban felt that neither a well-designed proscenium nor a simple black box theater was enough for the dance pieces he was creating. He sensed that the audience was not used to engaging with dance because most simply were unprepared, having not had the opportunity to see much dance. The audience's eye needed to be trained to see abstract group dance. Without such assistance, audience members see the scope and range but not the specific quality of the movement. Laban felt that the lack of education explained why people saw something merely acrobatic as art, a complaint echoed by dance artists before (Jean-George Noverre in the eighteenth century in his *Letters on Dancing and Ballet*) and since (see TV's *Dancing with the Stars*).

In one rant he said that since the dance theater staff had the task of discovering an appropriate space for the work along with finding an audience willing to really see and be open, a great deal of perspective, education in the discipline of dance performance, and a willingness to solve problems was required.

TANZTHEATER REFLECTED THE POLITICAL AND SOCIAL ISSUES OF THE TIMES

The technique developed by Laban and the Tanzbühne fed and informed his socially reflective commentary on everyday life and the populace's growing questions about power, community and violence in the latter half of the 1920s. The cinema, theater and cabarets produced work that was as dark and foreboding as it was wild, bitingly satirical and free-flowing. Fritz Lang's film *Metropolis* (1927) and the Brecht-Weill piece *Die Dreigroschenoper* (*The Threepenny Opera*) (1928) are examples of such work; both call into question capitalist as well as socialist ideals.

Brecht was writing and producing at this time, and even though his greatest fame was still to come, his ideas were part and parcel of the times. He promoted the notion that reason and logic ought to prevail over emotionality. His goal was social change, and in order to charge the audience into considering current circumstances, a certain amount of direct communication, if not detachment from illusion, was needed.

Brecht introduced the notion of epic theater, or theater that distances and objectifies the theatrical experience. In *Die Dreigroschenoper* (*The Threepenny Opera*), which opened in Berlin in 1928, characters commented on the scenes they were in, signage was used as commentary, harsh lighting overly illuminated the dark corners of the world of MacHeath and Jenny. The audience might be both seduced and charmed by MacHeath's cunning and sedition and alienated by them as well. Laban would have been aware of such techniques and used similar approaches to objectify and engage simultaneously.

To take one example, the character of "The Queen of the Night", a recurring archetype in his dance plays, and an ongoing shadow character in his life, was also the symbol for his ambivalence about the café society of the early 1900s and the decay of the 1920s. The model for the "Queen of the Night" came from an old Turkish tale; a story similar to that of both *Cinderella* and the *Sleeping Beauty*. She is the wise fairy who sees what the young heroine needs and who provides ancient knowledge and protection. Laban's sense of the Queen however, was more complicated and dark. The spirit of creativity and insight, the exploration of the depths of the soul, a concern with human follies and a willingness to intervene prevailed in his interpretation of the myth. But he also saw propensities for self-aggrandizement and narcissism.

The "Queen of the Night" was the all-consuming, larger-than-life, highly decorative, highly acquisitive prima donna. Laban knew that when people are inflated by the world and materiality, they can become grotesque. When such characters are also merely decorative (as opposed to expressive), they can be monsters. The Queens of the Night did not get to flourish by operating from a core of expressivity and good behavior. The archetype does not reflect wrenching self-examination or concern for mistakes made. As in Brecht's plays, and in Laban's *Nacht* (1927) the powerful Queen, represented by a variety of characters both male and female, watches carefully and has years of experience sizing people up quickly for their usefulness and efficacy. Laban used such characters in his dance plays and in so doing, he held up a somewhat ironic mirror of the times. Even in *The Green Clowns*, which was not one of his more somber works, the Club of the Weirdos section must have included such an overpowering reminder of his early days in Paris, when his romantic sensibilities were under-cut by the cynical sophistication of the overly decorated denizens of society.

Martin Gleisner, describing Laban's aesthetics some years later, wrote: "To strive too consciously for beauty would only achieve the opposite—ostentatious vanity contradicting the basic conception of the genuine dancer" (Gleisner, 1970, p. 10).

TANZTHEATER INFORMED AND WAS INFORMED BY OTHERS CREATING THEIR OWN APPROACHES

Ausdrucktanz (Expressionist Dance), and specifically the tanztheater, valued clarity and specificity: each moment was informed by, if not a linear tale, a decision about meaningfulness and preciseness. The flow of moments from one to the next did not subsume the precision, but allowed breath and life into the work.

One exception to the flow-based expressive movement of the period was the work of Oskar Schlemmer. Schlemmer had been a painter and sculptor-turned-theater artist at the Bauhaus, a school of art and architecture in Weimar and later, Dessau. Schlemmer's *Bauhaus Dances* consisted of dancers encased in costumes that exaggerated the human figure with helmets and rounded rubber suits. The emphasis was on geometry and space rather than flow and expressivity.

Schlemmer complained in a 1931 edition of *Schrifftanz* that his work had been misunderstood and mischaracterized. It was seen as denying the humanity of the dancer and masking the human form. He made the point that at the center of the geometric forms was the man, always. Schlemmer, like Laban, saw that clarity of form and space increased the awareness of individual expressivity, and turned chaos into order.

In another volume of *Schrifftanz* (1930), the editor, Alfred Schlee addressed the evolution of the Ausdrucktanz, or expressionists, into what he called "the New Dance." He wrote that the expressionists wanted to "raise the banner of art" in a mystical or religious way. But, he wrote, emotional upheaval easily becomes cliché. An awakening of both the human body and the communal can also come out of emotionality, but to reject ballet completely and only deal with the moment and with resulting rituals is a mistake. Both the raising of consciousness and the precision of technique are valuable to dance.

Laban would have argued that he was not sacrificing one for the other. The immediacy of the moment and any intermediacy between inspiration and realization were of value, and clarified the meaning.

Schlee, the editor of *Schrifftanz*, addressed the nationalism of German dance as well and wrote not of Aryan supremacy, but rather, an attempt to define a pan-European basis for the new dance forms. Thus the tanztheater transcended the national boundaries that were about to come into contention once again, reflecting the desire of the dancers to be artists of the world, as the Asconans had aspired to some twenty years prior. And as the Asconans also discovered, the power-mongering world would not support democratic globalism without clear economic benefits.

The years 1926–30 were personally difficult for Laban, coming after his fall from the stage and the stress of the Dance Congresses. Dussia was a difficult partner, and Laban's various schools were in transition. Dussia moved to Paris to open up a school there, and Laban combined and dissolved various programs as the economic conditions worsened. A somewhat manic darkness had set in to the European community. The most challenging period in western civilization began with chancy, sometimes dangerous activities surfacing in the cabarets and in the streets. What had been liberating and innovative a few years earlier—jazz music, free dance and the like—shifted into a noir sensibility.

The dance was no exception. Mary Wigman's *Totentmal*, a requiem for dead soldiers, based on a poem and in collaboration with Albert

Talhoff appeared in 1929. The piece was a large group opus, and Wigman wrote about the work:

> It was no longer a matter of the play of forces with and against one another ... The potential matter of conflict was no longer to be solved within the group itself. What was of concern here was the unification of a group of human beings [that] strove from a unified viewpoint toward a common aim recognized by everyone; a viewpoint which no longer permitted any splitting into single actions ...
>
> In the same way as the choric creation demands its antagonist—whether or not it takes actual shape or takes effect as thematic idea above and beyond the events—in many cases it also asks for a leader [*Anführer*] chosen by the chorus, for the one who conveys the message powerfully, who, supported and carried by the entire chorus, advances the thematic idea and brings it to its final execution.

(Wigman, 1966, pp. 92–93)

Wigman's words are ominous, but make sense within the context of Germany in the late 1920s. Boundaries were being broken regularly on social and artistic levels, and a growing awareness that imposed order might be a relief from the roller coaster economic conditions began to prevail.

TANZTHEATER BROKE OLD RULES AND CREATED NEW ONES

Through the entire spectra of possibilities, Rudolf Laban teased out a new way of creating dance works, a way that embraced seeming contradictions and brought polar ends back together to complete a circle of possibilities. There was no rule that could not be broken, and no dichotomy that could not be mended. In fact, it was always the tensions between and among ideas, points in space, positions, dogmas and expressive moments that made the dance artful.

Laban was, at the core, a craftsman and an explorer of approaches. Because he was at heart an improviser, he liked blasting through boundaries and trying things in new ways. For each piece he created, he devised a vocabulary and style. His process was to begin with an idea, often an archetypal story or setting, then to derive a vocabulary for that time and place. The dancers explored actively, and he selected from their array, much as he did for his 1929 crafts festival in Vienna.

He was also a recycler of material. He was both pragmatic and opportunistic, in the sense of being able to make the best out of a situation. Without needing to adorn, he explored and took what was available, making the best of it. As a keen observer, he saw things that needed to come to fruition, and he was able to tease out the essentials.

Dörr (Interview, July 9, 2004) points out that tanztheater covered many different genres and styles. "*Don Juan* could be performed by the chamber group alone or with a choir. Laban recycled sections over and over. *Orchidée* may in fact have been derived from a section of *The Swinging Temple*."

Laban added the local movement choir groups (mostly amateur but trained in improvisation) to works if they were appropriate and available. This flexibility was both a financial necessity and part of his choreographic principles.

THE GREEN CLOWNS/DIE GRÜNEN CLOWNS AS TANZTHEATER

Against this complex backdrop, over four years, Laban's work, *Die Grünen Clowns* developed. It was described as an ironic comment on human behavior, in contrast to Wigman's *Totenmal*, which was portrayed as a powerful communion of the soul and death. As early as 1926, the artistic differentiation between Laban and Wigman had become evident, leading critics and audiences alike to choose sides. Laban's work, especially following the fall from the stage in Don Juan (in 1926) that ended his performing career, moved away from the experimental and toward the epic, but with a sense of irony. Wigman was becoming a well-known artist with particularly trained dancers behind her. Laban's approach allowed for the trained and less-trained dancers to enter into building work with a sense of community.

It is important to remember that in his time, Laban was considered a master choreographer and the "Father of German Modern Dance." Even though none of his works survive in any wholly replicable form, his approach to choreography is precisely how many twenty-first century contemporary artists work with their dancers. The manipulation of movement into abstract but specifically expressive moments, and the dance director who is more of a guide than a scriptwriter are both familiar to us now. Laban also learned a great deal from his lovers and dancers, especially Perrottet and Bereska, both more traditionally trained as dancers than he himself was, and both willing to share their own insights into the technical execution of particular movement.

Die Grünen Clowns appears to have begun life as a satiric piece, part of a larger set of such pieces, in 1926. Laban structured it with Dussia Bereska, his muse and partner of that period. It was not in the category of exotic or decorative dances; it was meant to be grotesque, a pantomime depicting Laban and Bereska's observations of contemporary society.

Exotic dances were those that addressed the period's fascination with "Orientalism", as in *Orchidée*. Decorative dances would have been expressive works without deeper meaning; Laban was not interested in such as these.

THE GROTESQUE

An agent of transgression, the grotesque is always on the verge of transforming, demanding "the furtive glance rather than the rapacious gaze." He (Remshart) divides the grotesque into "weak" and "strong" categories that depend on the perception of the viewer, his or her cultural and moral assumptions at any given time.

(Robb, 2005, pp. 856–858)

The grotesque yokes the trivial and the demonic. It establishes "a co-presence of the ludicrous with the monstrous, the disgusting or the horrifying" (Thomson, Philip. *The Grotesque*. London: Methuen, 1972). Exaggeration, hyperbole and excessiveness are fundamental attributes of the grotesque style, according to Bakhtin (Bakhtin, Mikhail, *Rabelais and His World*. Trans. Helen Iswolsky. Bloomington: Indiana UP, 1984, p. 301), who argued that "the central principle of grotesque realism is degradation, that is, the lowering of all that is high, spiritual, ideal."

(Wasserman, 2004, pp. 33–37)

In the sense that grotesque dance is transgressive, or undermining of social expectations, mores and values, Laban's aesthetic for *The*

Green Clowns lies firmly in that category. It was a commentary on the society of the time; it was social satire and the creators were not above using the more confrontational style of hyperbole to get the points across.

The relationship between "clown" and "monster" must have been tangible even before the mid-1920s, but by the time *The Green Clowns* made its debut, the connection was present and portended what was to come, in the too-bright cabarets of Berlin and the rise of fascism via a man who was perceived first as a clown and later as a monster. Laban's earlier character of the Queen of the Night fell into the category of the grotesque, and although she did not make an appearance in this work (at least as far as is known), clowns/monsters reminiscent of her did.

One can imagine the work as an exploration of the fine line between the two. One can also imagine that it showed the two as two sides of the same coin, or two facets of contemporary leaders.

The sequence and content changed over the two years (1926–28) that the piece was in the forefront of the Tanzbühne Repertory. At its premiere in 1926 at the Schillertheater Hamburg-Altona, there were ten clowns; that is all we know about it, as there were no reviews. The sections, according to Evelyn Dörr (Interview, July 9, 2004), were as follows:

1 Psychomechanik
2 Verkettungen (connections, chains)
3 Klub der Sonderlinge (Club of the Weirdos)
4 Gedankenflucht (solo—escaping from one's thoughts—daydreaming)
5 Firlefanz (silliness, frivolous stuff—junk, fluffiness, frippery, clowning around)
6 Zeitlupe (slow motion—five clowns)
7 Militarismus (group)
8 Atonale (atonal)

This first sequence of eight sections does not appear to develop an idea or through line so much as present a smorgasbord of shifting rhythms and group sizes. It may be that these were early effort studies, or experiments with qualities. The structure of the piece also suggests that it was designed (to the extent that it was designed) to be performed in a variety of types of spaces. Laban clearly valued the large mythic works that required appropriate stage space, with room for platforms and set pieces, but he also had to solve the challenges of the touring chamber group, and *The Green Clowns* would have been adaptable enough to fit into many spaces that the larger works would not have.

In 1927, Laban gave a new name to the work: *Grotesque in sechs Bewegungen* (*Grotesque in six movements*). The sequence apparently changed and several sections got new names as well:

1 Maschine
2 Romanze in Grün (Green romance)
3 Gedankenflucht (solo—escaping from one's thoughts—daydreaming)

Maschine was another in a long line of Laban statements about the rise of industrialism, and included some nonverbal commentary on the loss of individual enterprise and creativity.

Zeitlupe, Romanze in Grün and Gedankenflucht may have been slower reflections on man's ideals and romantic notions, and the ultimate fatalism of romance. The Klub der Sonderlinge makes sense within the cabaret scene of the time, with its slow descent into darker themes, but it also clearly refers to the grotesque style of undermining the status quo that characterized the clown/monster archetype.

At some point in 1927, a scene called "Spuk" (spook) appeared that consisted of six clowns doing simultaneous movement: one figure facing the audience, with five others with their back to the audience. Press reviews from that time said that scene was "terrific" (from the newspaper NZZ, May 7, 1927). The image is not dissimilar to the line of masked figures moving along in Wigman's *Totenmal* (1930), and has a touch of Brechtian alienation.

By 1928, at the Choreographical Institute Berlin, with music by Erich Itor Kahn, eight sections had emerged, with another new name: *Grotesque mit sechs Clowns* (*Grotesque with Six Clowns*).

It would appear that the clown motif had taken over and become more of the foreground of the through line by this version. The characters of fools, or clowns, trying to get on in a mad world seems to have become the major theme by this time and the question arises as to whether the clowns were perpetrators of the mad world, or victims? The fact that the seventh section, Militarismus, appears only in the early 1926 version, and then disappears from subsequent versions, lends some support to the clown motif taking over from the anti-technology motifs of the earlier version.

Later on in 1928, the sequence changed again; new sections were added:

- Nachtigall (nightingale)
- Gehirnoperation (brain surgery)
- So ist das Leben (That's Life!)
- Five O'clock (a trio, with music by Boris Blacher)

No doubt sections came and went, and versions abounded. The appearance of a new section did not mean that that section was kept, or even performed every time. It may be that Laban added and subtracted sections for many reasons, including who was around to dance that particular performance.

In one version, a dancer brought a little door out onto the stage that he went through, after which he cleaned himself with little brushes. In the Gehirnoperation (brain surgery) section (1928), one dancer mimed screwing off the head of the other and taking the brains out, foreshadowing Marcel Marceau and hundreds of street mimes yet to come. One wonders what might have become of the "brains" in performance, given the context of the grotesque.

According to Dörr (Interview, July 9, 2004), it's also possible that some parts of *Narrenspiegel* (*Fool's Mirror*) were taken and/or given to the *Green Clowns*. Such recycling would have been in keeping with the evolving scenes of clowns or fools trying to negotiate a crazy world, as well as Laban's propensity for improvisation and (by necessity, if not choice) frugality. Press reviews from the time said that all sections, scenery and ideas were grotesque and over the top, which was a positive statement.

Photographs from the period of the piece reveal dancers with a clear sense of space, lots of exaggerated expression, and shaping among the clowns as they are strewn about each other. The grotesque aesthetic Laban espoused did not mean a lack of clarity; on the other hand, it was not realistic movement either. From the photos, not a shred of muddiness or compromise in expression is apparent, in keeping with Laban and Bereska's values of specificity and potency.

Clearly, over time the piece grew, evolved, expanded and shrank; sections were added and others deleted. The piece was alive in temporal, spatial and ever-shifting responsive ways; just like Laban saw human movement itself. The work may have been unique in its fluidity of structure: audiences may have had vastly differing experiences from one night to the next, but it reflected the increasing tensions and sense of dark absurdity of the late 1920s.

As many of his dance-plays were, *The Green Clowns* was a devised work that comprised original moments that formed a specific vocabulary and meaning which served that dance work alone. In this sense, the dance was pure Expressionism, and helped to further define Laban's notion of tanztheater.

Valerie Preston-Dunlop has set about to recreate the work, using Laban's typical approaches to gleaning movement from the dancers. With only the sketchiest of reviews and photos, and from her memory of working with Laban in the latter half of the 1940s, she managed to derive a full piece that, seemingly, deals with the same issues, themes and approaches to movement as Laban. The piece has the look and feel of a tanztheater work, and she has captured some of the grotesque aesthetic, especially, the attitude of artifice and exaggeration of shape and space.

The process is one of guided improvisation. Dancers need to be trained in Laban-based dance approaches, which would include Effort and Space work, in order to use the "Schwingen" (swinging) and expressive aspects of the work, but once the through line and themes are determined, the movement itself would resemble the photos and descriptions from the times.

It is likely that the aesthetic Laban developed for the piece fed both his systematic approach to movement analysis, providing categories for expressive movement and spatial configurations; and a freewheeling, problem-solving attitude towards the construction of new works that we see in later choreographic processes throughout the twentieth century. From Cunningham to Judson to Pilobolus, each used an approach to choreography that involved solving a problem or defying conventions of one kind or another.

From *The Green Clowns*, twenty-first-century artists can recall and recapitulate the legacies of improvisation, innovation, exaggeration, regeneration and reflection of ever-changing times. The form Laban used of sections of dance-based social commentary became a key element of works that followed, including Kurt Jooss' *The Green Table*.

That work, *The Green Table*, shares more than themes of social commentary with *The Green Clowns*. The color green is significant in several disciplines, the most obvious of which is ecology or environmental studies. The relationship between man and the physical world, or Mother Nature, is dynamic and reciprocal, and the color green appears to have some deep and ancient connection to that relationship.

Green is also the color of gambling and game tables, or platforms for man's follies. Certainly, the notion of the poker table was one of the significant influences on Jooss' title. Laban's use of the color is less obvious, and it seems also to have been mutable. If one goes back to Kandinsky's theories of color, which Laban would have known about, green is a color of restful complacency, hardly adding to the meaning inherent in either work.

But if green is a table or platform and a background color for man's follies, then the choice is intriguing: a cool underpinning for foibles and heartbreak, for madness and absurdity.

Other elements the pieces shared include irony and the use of the grotesque especially to depict characters of power. Jooss' figure of Death, the Gentlemen in Black, and the Profiteer would all be recognizable evolutions of the grotesque clowns in Laban's work especially those in *The Green Clowns*. Whereas Laban's clowns were not assigned particular roles to play—they were, apparently, just generic clowns—Jooss' grotesque characters took on specific roles and duties. However, all the clown/monster characters in both Laban's and Jooss' work deal with the trivial and the monstrous simultaneously.

The use of tensions, or opposites, in space and expression was also a common mode in both works. In the surviving piece, one can sense the wit and depth of the lost work, for Jooss himself paid homage to Laban's guidance as a director. The coaching of dancers for specificity and clarity of space and expression is a significant part of any restaging of Jooss' masterpiece, and is as apparent in recent reconstructions as the photos of Laban's work from the late 1920s demonstrate.

While *Die Grünen Clowns* was not a piece that remained in memory in the way that *The Green Table* has, and rightly so, the elements and point of view that Laban's work used informed the genre that Jooss was developing at the time, and supported the ingenuity of both men. And there can be little doubt that teacher and student drank from the same wells, and fed each other.

TANZTHEATER'S LEGACY

The tanztheater left a lasting legacy. To this day, mature contemporary dance work contains clear and meaningful moments of specific expression, whether the moment be a sideways glance, a throwing motion, a fall to the floor, a sniff at the air, or a turning away from one another. Postural shifts and tiny gestures resonate to the back rows of the audience when effort is clarified and supported by the core of the dancer's body. Movement can be large and stylized and yet detailed and potent. The legacy of the tanztheater is that generalizations do not carry; delineations communicate.

But all is not literal. In the work Laban created, the idiosyncratic and the abstract played a role. Characters have details as well as unique predilections that can be exploited and even abstracted to a point of unrecognizability and still retain clear focus. Human stories are not necessarily linear or logical, but can still be compelling.

Improvisation yields sometimes-irrational impulses, around which stories of human foibles can be woven and the absurd can be made rational, or at least understandable. Shining light on absurdity is a way of laughing in the light at our all-too-human follies.

And yet, the darker passions of mankind and the dissolution of society that leads in and out of violence are also fodder for the dance theater of today. We have our own stable of grotesque characters and situations to be sure, but such is the richness of human imagination that archetypes are recognizable, no matter what medium they appear in. Contemporary dance work makes good use of the darker side of human souls and issues like war, exploitation and betrayal are still part of the scene.

Materials and ideas are not one shot deals and just as Laban recycled phrases, costumes and images from one piece to another, contemporary artists embrace the act of retooling older ideas and borrowing images and techniques from one another in order to create truly original versions of the stories we keep telling ourselves. It is a form of sustainability and a shortcut to recognition of pattern.

And finally, audiences in Laban's time began to realize that they had choices about how to take in the work they were seeing and they could engage at personal levels, perhaps even participate. He gave permission for dance to be both virtuosic and accessible; he used pedestrian movement as well as abstract and remote images.

What we appear to have lost, however, is the use of tension and counter-tensions to highlight the internal dramas of human beings. Such angst-ridden movement appears old-fashioned to us nowadays and the value of releasing over containing, of discharging over selecting has given dancers a virtuosic fierceness but not a richness of scope and depth. Dance training is, all too often, an approaching process rather than a gathering process. The creation process for choreography draws on the eclecticism and improvisation-based approaches Laban developed, but the exploration of dramatic conflicts internally and in social contexts through the movement itself has often been abandoned. The pendulums always swing back, so perhaps his idea of physically negotiating oppositional pulls will return when we decide we need the warmth that friction provides.

This bold approaching of the dream life is what the artist truly does ... Art is a sublimation and condensation of this piecemeal insertion of the so-called irrational sparks and impulses into all thoughts and actions.

(From *Laban Speaks*, a lecture given in London April 1957, p. 4)

4

MASTERY OF MOVEMENT FOR THE TWENTY-FIRST-CENTURY PERFORMER

From a morning stretch to a hip-hop spin; from a politician's gesture to an infant's crawling patterns; from standards in learning in the arts to observation of psychiatric patients, Laban's legacy continues to inform and challenge us in performance and everyday life. The tanz-theater, notation, the physical preparation for expressive movement, the healing practices, the work in education and industry, actor preparation and movement design are all pertinent to the twenty-first-century performer and practitioner.

Laban's source material came from physics and philosophy, the cultural and counter-cultural practices of his times, medicine and psychology, visual art and music, and so too do the contemporary applications of his work. In the twenty-first century, the utility of Laban's work to dance, theater, communications studies, discourse analysis, therapy, critical analysis, health, and similar fields is growing.

BODY LANGUAGE OR MOVEMENT LANGUAGE?

Every little movement does not have a meaning of its own, but every little movement means something to the mover, and therefore resonates (or does not resonate) for the audience of the mover. Interpretation is often tricky because as observers, people impose personal and cultural perspectives and beliefs onto the observation. We live in a multicultural and complicated world and so miscommunications are common. No performer, no matter how much training he/she has had, is completely neutral either. Any time we communicate, we are, in a way, performing for an audience, and therefore we are attempting to be clear with meaning. Laban's approach shows us that we can develop a greater repertoire of possible configurations, clarify the baseline of movement patterns with which we are already comfortable, and observe and embody other patterns that convey different qualities and configurations.

In the popular culture, the term "body language" is often used to describe the analysis of signs and symbols within nonverbal communication. But Laban Movement Analysis (LMA) is not a systematic way of interpreting movement as signs or symbols of particular meaning. Rather, LMA sees movement patterns as personally and/or culturally significant. In other words, crossing one's arms in front of the torso does not always mean the same thing. There are personal aspects, contextual cues (is it cold out?) and cultural aspects that inform any interpretation.

THE BIG PICTURE

Our language is full of dichotomies: these splits reflect our inability culturally to reconcile self and other, function and expression, sacred and profane aspects of human life, and every other divisive approach to understanding the nature of human behavior. LMA directly addresses the integration of polar opposites. In fact, if there is a core value of LMA, it is the union of opposites. LMA reflects the beliefs of Laban and his followers that each element of movement has polar ends, but what is significant is the nature of the element as a whole. At the same time, it is important to clarify polar ends categorically, in order to tease apart the unique qualities of the entire spectrum.

LMA offers this gift, but is also judged by this gift. A key example of the ways in which LMA clarifies and unites concepts is that LMA is both a research approach and a somatics practice. As such, it defies categorization, at least in the traditional sense of categories as exclusive. In our culture, methodologies are either research/scholarly/empirical forms of inquiry or they are practical experiences and growth processes. The idea that LMA can be both at the same time is not easy to grasp, especially for those inside the academy.

Yet the reconciliation of theory and practice is rooted in the history of Laban Movement Analysis, from Ascona to Vienna to Dartington to Addlestone to New York City. Each center of thought also informed practices, and vice versa. To this day, the training of Certified Movement Analysts takes place on studio floors, in nearby parks and other public spaces, and in the media lab. The values and beliefs of the early twentieth-century enlightenment period, in which science and art were aspects of human understanding, continue to play out in the early twenty-first century.

Movement mediates inner and outer experiences, another dichotomy that LMA integrates. The themes of LMA also include exertion/recuperation, function/expression, and stability/mobility. Each polar end of the continua defines and informs the opposite end, providing full experiences of our bodies in motion and interaction with the world.

Exertion/recuperation: Culturally we are busy people, more and more so each day. It is difficult to tell whether the amount of energy expended on any number of mental tasks exceeds the amount of physical work our ancestors had to do, or if the work is just performed using different body parts. Whatever the amount of energy however, what is reduced is leisure time: time to reflect and dream. Laban understood the need for a balance overall between tension and release, work and play. But balance is not an absolute place or position; rather, it is a dynamic interplay along a continuum. The overall effect of such interaction between work and play, and exercise and repose, is to provide a personal sense of balance; one that is different for each individual. One man's coping mechanism may be handball or racquetball, while another's may be listening to symphony music. One woman might find food shopping recuperative, while another takes a yoga class. The exertion/recuperation continuum provides an array of coping mechanisms for the craziness of contemporary life.

When working with clients or students on issues of overwork or overuse, the notion of exertion/recuperation is useful and often, novel. People who are regularly rewarded for overworking find the notion of balance challenging, but it is essential to mental and physical health.

Function/expression: Contemporary culture also overvalues functional movement (related to task completion) over expressive or purely communicative movement behavior. And yet, one so often informs the other. Certain tasks require an ability to alter the quality of one's movement, and expressive movement often requires a change in function in order to execute a particular skill. Construction work, for example, requires movers who can access strong weight effort in order to overcome and mobilize the weight of large pieces of equipment. At the same time, ballet requires a high degree of technical prowess and functionality. Function and expression are not, therefore, dichotomous, but rather shadings of movement that often co-exist.

Stability / Mobility: One of the most subtle truths about leadership is the ability that successful CEOs and politicians have to come across as both stabilizing and mobilizing actors. A leader who is only stable, as in taking a position that is static, cannot lead people into transition or change. A leader who is only mobile, as in hard to pin down, may not give confidence to followers and may appear to be "flighty." The idea that leadership requires both stability and mobility is one that leaders often understand intuitively, but it is actual movement practice that gives direct experience of both that allows true comprehension and clear communication.

LABAN MOVEMENT ANALYSIS

The categories that Laban derived (Body, Effort, Space) have been expanded to include a category he wrote about but did not identify as a separate category: Shape. Shape is a late-twentieth-century category developed by Warren Lamb, a protégé of Laban's. It addresses the changing relationship of the mover to him/herself and/ or an object outside the self. The entire system can be viewed as a tetrahedron:

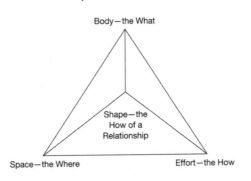

The tetrahedron reveals the structure of a movement "sentence," or phrase. A person moves an arm, up, with lightness, bridging to a point, for example. Such a moment has clarity, expressivity and connection. There are millions of possible combinations of body, effort, shape and space, but not all movers utilize all four categories equally. It is the patterns that an individual uses expressively and functionally, over and over again, that define individual style. As performers evolve into characters, finding the character's style becomes key to revealing the character's story. Laban's categories offer both a map and taxonomy for discovering style.

THE BODY LEVEL

What is moving? What body parts are active? Passive? Tense? How does the body organize itself sequentially or spatially? What actions are taken by which body parts? The photographs below offer a simple illustration of the kinds of body level choices a performer can make to bring character into sharper focus.

Laban Movement Analysis treats body parts, body actions (running, walking, jumping, etc.) and body organization as arising from the same basic precepts categorically. Active body parts, activities and events, and the intrapsychic organization for those tasks comprise the subject and the verb of the movement "sentence."

Everything arises from breath, especially the tri-phasic inspiration/transaction/expression sequence of the breathing, or respiration process. Human beings take in breath as a gathering up of the environment. Inspiration, the taking in of breath, is therefore a form of nourishment. It is followed by an internal transaction, an exchange of gases that is a type of digestion. The unneeded gases are expelled or expressed. Without the need to communicate emotions, language or sensations to others, this process would be merely functional and unchanging. But it is our need to clarify and communicate that informs the rate, pace and qualities of the respiration cycle. We gasp, or we spew in exasperation, or we sigh or sob, or we hold our breath in waiting, and all of it informs the voice.

We also communicate metaphorically and experientially from body parts: hearts sink or are worn on the sleeve, brains are fried, we haven't the stomach for something, we speak off the top of the head, we are armed or disarmed, or we try to get a leg up—our language reflects the varied and symbolic ways we understand ourselves through our bodies.

Laban's approach to training the body was essentially an exploration of possibilities. Exercises consisted of growing and shrinking, taking in breath and releasing it from a general experience of whole body movement through a process of refining and discovering qualities and directions, tensions and releases, clarifying the movement with both precision and subtleties.

Figure 4.1 Two in discussion from head energy

Figure 4.2 Two in discussion from heart energy

Figure 4.3 Speaking from the gut

The movers in his classes performed phrases of steps and shapes, but these were explorations of meaningful movement and developments of ideas that arose in the class itself. He discovered much of the analysis of body attitude, body actions and body part usage through the teaching process.

Laban understood the profound levels of body movement and the rich images that arise from action and access. But it was his student Irmgard Bartenieff who integrated Laban's understanding of body and meaning with somatics and physical rehabilitation practices.

The experiential practice of body level concepts such as connection, sequencing, support, and organization is called Bartenieff Fundamentals [sm]. The principles that underlie the Fundamentals can be practiced and utilized for better vocal support, clearer communication of message, greater efficiency and endurance, deeper meaningfulness and expressivity, and more effective patterns.

Practice

Access: The above photos represent access to particular areas of the body that are meaningful communicatively. Movement that originates from particular areas of the body, such as the head, heart and gut, help get one's points across in richer ways.

Each of us has preferential patterns: parts of the body that are easy to access, and parts that seem to be acting independently of our personality. A politician, who speaks from the head, radiating intellectual substance, may come across as either newly emotional or insincere when he suddenly begins speaking from his heart. A soldier, who operates from his gut, by necessity, might find himself with sudden access to his head energy when he has to think on his feet and communicate strategy.

How can one develop access so that one has choices? Step one is simply to breathe into each area—expanding with the inhale (inspiration), and condensing with exhalation (expression). Adding vocalizations to the exhalation phase can clarify the particular qualities that are associated with each area and provide even more access. Try exhaling from the head center with an eeeeee sound, the heart with a rounded aaahhhh sound, and the gut with an open ohhhhhh sound.

Another layer of access: practice movement phrases or short scenes from each center and note how the messages are different for each.

And a third layer: have a conversation with someone speaking completely from one of the centers: head, heart, gut. What happened in the course of the conversation?

Release of Tension: We all hold tension in certain parts of the body. In many cases the tension is dysfunctional and a result of old beliefs or patterns that we no longer need. In some cases, the tension is functional and adaptive, in the case of injury or in the service of conveying intensity. In Laban's tanztheater, tension and the ability to shift tensions and to utilize changing tensions were key to communicating the human dramas and commentary. In all cases, the ability to increase and relieve tension consciously is useful.

The Heel-Rock, which is a part of the Bartenieff Fundamentals^sm, can be used to both identify and relieve tension. This exercise can be done standing or lying on the floor. Begin with flexions and extensions in the ankle joint in a rocking rhythm; allow the flow of the rhythm and the rocking to sequence into the knee joints, the hips and pelvis, along the spine, and into the point at which the spine enters the skull (the occipital). The goal is to allow the body to release into full rocking and sequencing, opening the breath, releasing the shoulders and rib cage, and connecting up the vertical architecture of the body.

Connections: In our disconnected world, where reality appears to be located inside a screen and people have a difficult time experiencing their own bodies, it makes sense that some remedial building of sensation from body part to body part would be useful. Connections in the Bartenieff work are much more than anatomical; movement requires dynamic chains.

The head-tail connection is the core connector, transcending the typical upper-lower body disconnections. In a culture in which the legs are used to locomote and the rest of the functional and expressive work of the body takes place from the waist, or even the shoulders, up, reconnecting dynamically can allow the mover to be versatile and adaptive.

Other body level connections that often require attention include the heel-sit bone and the scapula-hand connections. The heel-sit bone connection allows for proper sequencing of the heel-to-pelvis walking pattern, as well as supporting the body in elevation. The scapula-hand connection is critical for both full expressivity (as in dance performance) of the upper body as well as the prevention of the various syndromes associated with computer, PDA and video game overuse.

Sequencing: Rolling down and up the spine is a good way to begin to experience the kind of sequencing that builds dynamic connections in the core of the body. Many modern dance and movement for actors' classes use the spinal rolls as a basic approach to voice and dance technique. Yoga uses spinal rolls as well. In the Laban/Bartenieff work, the spinal rolls are both profound and assimilating, providing depth and integration of movement and allowing for support for space and expression.

Sequencing through the scapula-hand connection is yet another profound experience. Lying on one's back, with the arms spread, initiate with the finger tips of one hand and sequence movement, tracking with the fingertips leading, across the midline of the body to the opposite arm, still spread. Follow visually. Return the moving arm back to where it began by initiating with the scapula. Repeat with the other arm. The exercise is useful as recuperation from typing or entering data as well as for young children who have difficulty tracking movement visually or in crossing the midline of the body. (Crossing the midline is a priori to learning to read, to forming letters or to drawing. It is also useful for ball sports and is required for pitching or accurately kicking a ball.)

Support: In addition to breath support, which underlies and informs every part of human movement, other parts of the body are more or less designed to provide support for human functioning and can be used to clarify expressivity as well. The floor of the pelvis (called the uro-genital triangle) is a diaphragm. This diaphragm supports the organs of the lower pelvis and must be elastic enough to both support a fetus and allow for birth in women. The pelvic floor can initiate forward, upward, backward, sideways and downward movement. When movement initiates from such a core place, it is efficient and specific. The pelvic floor shifts the lower and upper halves of the body in a kinetic chain, and the body organizes itself sequentially.

The thoracic diaphragm also supports organs, in this case the lungs and heart. It must also be both strong and resilient. The diaphragm attaches to the spine at the bottom of the thoracic vertebrae, which is the same vertebrae at which the top end of the iliopsoas muscle group attaches as well. The iliopsoas is a vertically oriented muscle group deep within the core of the lower half of the torso. Ultimately a hip flexor, the psoas connects and supports the upper and lower body-halves.

To engage in a variety of ways of supporting the body through the pelvic diaphragm, the thoracic diaphragm and the iliopsoas, the first three exercises of the Basic Six fundamentals are appropriate. These are the *Thigh Flexion*, the *Pelvic Lateral Shift* and the *Pelvic Forward Shift*.

The *Thigh Flexion* is done on the back, with both knees bent and feet on the floor. On an exhale, the psoas is engaged in a lengthening and deepening of the abdominal muscles and this flexes the hip joint so that the leg is lifted off the floor. The leg remains bent and the lower part of the leg should not droop, but should be supported with a heel-sit bone dynamic connection. The leg returns to the beginning position (knee bent, foot on the floor, also on an exhale. It may help to vocalize while exhaling in order to keep the breath open and the movement smooth.

The *Pelvic Lateral Shift* is initiated by a deepening exhalation and lengthening of the psoas as well, but instead of the hips flexing so one leg is lifted off the floor, the pelvis lifts straight up, while the upper body remains on the floor. The feet are planted and stabilize the lower half, while the pelvis is raised just a few inches off the floor. With the pelvis still off the floor, a shift of the pelvic diaphragm in a straight line from the trochanter to either the right or left, on a horizontal line parallel to the floor begins. When the anatomical limit has been reached, the pelvis lowers to the floor. Then the pelvis is lifted, slides back to the midline and is lowered back to the floor. The entire phrase repeats on the opposite side of the body. It is important to stand up after this exercise and walk around the room, noting the additional support of the pelvic floor for lateral weight shifts, creating a natural Latin or Caribbean sway.

The *Pelvic Forward Shift* begins the same way as the lateral shift, but another forward movement is added to the raising of the pelvis; a thrusting forward and up off the floor in a reverse ski slope movement. It is the on-the-floor movement equivalent of a demi-plie, with a slight forward tilt of the pelvis added. The thoracic spine remains on the floor during this exercise. One helpful image is to think about the two pelvic sit bones and the pelvic diaphragm being pulled forward and up at the same time, with a quick initiation.

After the *Thigh Flexion, Pelvic Lateral* and *Pelvic Forward Shift* have been practiced, walking around the room or climbing stairs is a different experience for most. The legs feel more connected to both the torso and the ground, and the access to movement in all directions is increased. Often people enjoy simple bouncing, kicking, a little samba dancing, etc. after these exercises.

The voice changes as well. These exercises open up the lower vocal channels and allow for deeper tonality and power.

Grounding: The exercises above all yield a profoundly felt sense of connectivity with the earth and gravity. The connections one experiences are not passive or tense, but dynamic and rich. Groundedness is a powerful state of being for many reasons, but two relate directly to Rudolf Laban's theories. Laban believed that the organic or biological world influences and is influenced by the world of objects and devised structures. People adapt to the environment at the same time that they act on the environment, and the dynamic systems of body and earth adapt whenever encounters happen.

Overcoming gravity as a pull, as in a jump, is an example of human will and technique modulating in a dynamic way with the forces of the universe. A grounded mover entering a room or the stage can execute expressive and communicative movement far better than a mover who is not fully engaged with either gravity or the surface of the space in a dynamic way. At the same time, Laban also understood the value of the empowered mover, the individual who can adapt to the environment and the community while remaining grounded in himself.

Counter-tension: Another concept that Irmgard drew on from Laban's theories was that of polarities united. Grounding is richer and more potent when there is a corresponding pull out into space, through the core of the body. The anatomy of the body supports counter-tensions in a variety of directions, of which the arabesque is but one example. Counter-tension is the gift of motion to position, illustrating the laws of stability and mobility. Polar ends of the body, or of an idea, are not disconnected from each other, but rather exist along a continuum of tensions, releases, interactions and dynamic interplay. Stability informs mobility and vice versa.

A good way to experience this concept is to work with three people. One person lies on the floor on his/her back in an X position, with arms and legs extended away from the center of gravity. One helper sits by one hand of the person on the floor, and the other sits by the opposite foot. The helpers pick up the hand and foot and gently pull on the limbs until they feel the pull from the other end of the dynamic line of energy. Beginning to tug and release, they can set up a contralateral rocking along the diagonal line, allowing for the pull of the polar ends to take over eventually as they drop the hand and opposing foot and allow the mover to take over the awareness. Repeat on the other side and then switch movers and helpers. It is also useful to stand up after both contralateral diagonals have been engaged and to try some forms of counter-tension, either a held moment of extension in more than one direction, or in partnership with another, a la Contact Improvisation.

Organization: Gravity is the primary organizing principle of body and space; without it, one would not develop a sense of midline. The vertical midline of the body is informed by gravity. It divides the body into right and left halves. Indeed, when learning a new movement skill, humans tend to revert to a right-left organization. Think of the creeping pattern in infants, or the toddling walk of a young child. Both of these patterns are homolateral, or based in body-half organization.

In a sedentary culture, people do not get much of a chance to practice the homolateral patterning. Too many spend too much time in chairs or sitting in other ways, so that the organization that emerges is one of an upper-lower, or bilateral organization. In other words, the upper half of the body tends to operate separately from the lower half of the body. The homolateral organization is an essential precursor to contralateral organization, in ways that the upper/lower patterning is not. Therefore, practicing homolateral organization can be remedial and useful in reconnecting the upper and lower halves of the body.

The fourth Bartenieff Fundamental exercise of the Basic Six, *Body Half*, begins on the floor, with the mover lying on his/her back, in an X position. Arms and legs are extended away from the center of gravity. The right elbow and the right knee flex and move towards each other, and then recover back to the extended positions. It is not necessary for the elbow and knee to touch; they merely approach each other and then return to the original position. Repeat on the other side of the body.

The next phase is to add a folding over of the second half of the body, while the first half is in flexion. The right side elbow and knee initiate in flexion at the same time, moving toward each other and allowing the torso to bend toward the moving side. While the right side is condensed, the left arm and leg extend away from each other along the floor, and then the left hand and left foot initiate an arc, leading the entire left half of the body into a folding over of the left half over the right half. Recover to the beginning X position and repeat on the other side,

Eventually this body half exercise can take the mover into rolling over and over, extending a little as he/she opens up and folding more deeply as the roll intensifies.

The experience of rolling on the floor by slightly widening and narrowing through each body half can be applied to turns while standing. Pirouettes, barrel turns and chainé turns are all examples of basic body half organization, vertical midline crossing movement experiences that can be clarified and refined from the body-half fundamental exercise.

Contralateral organization uses the diagonal anatomical connections, including the internal and external oblique abdominal muscles, the latissimus dorsi and trapezius muscles of the back, and the sterno-cleidoid mastoid muscle of the neck. Support for a more sophisticated organization and for counter-tension can be facilitated by the combination of the fifth and sixth Basic Six fundamental exercises, the *Knee-Drop* into the *Arm Circle*.

The *Knee Drop* is done from the same on-the-back, on-the floor position as the first four of the Basic Six exercises, with knees bent and feet flat, placed at a distance as far apart as the sit bones and the arms out to the sides of the body. Each knee initiates separately from the other, but they drop towards the same side, allowing a spiraling sequence to roll through the pelvis and torso, along the diagonals, until the arm that is on the opposite side of the body rotates away from the direction the knees are dropping. The arm stays in the shoulder socket and the head turns toward the rotating arm. As a result, the body is in a spiral on the floor.

The *Arm Circle* initiates from the hand of the arm that is rotated away from the knees, or it can initiate from the shoulder joint, or the base of the scapula. Wherever it initiates from, the arm makes a complete circle, with elbow soft and not locked, either clockwise or counter-clockwise. As the arm passes over the diagonal midline (knees through the obliques, through the latissimus, the shoulder joint and the opposite arm) the torso needs to accommodate the movement through shaping support. The circle can be reversed (if the mover went clockwise the first time, he/she can go counter-clockwise next).

Recovering from both the *Knee Drop* and the *Arm Circle* can be initiated from the distal ends (knees or hands) or from the proximal joints (hips or shoulders) or from the core of the torso (through breath release/expression). Wherever the initiation comes from, both arms and legs return to the originating position on the back, with knees bent and arms spread.

After repeating the entire sequence on the other diagonal midline or side of the body, it is useful to stand up (slowly) and walk around the room, trying both counter-tension positions as well as mobilizing sequences such as slides, tours-jetés, spirals to the floor and up again, and other examples of three-dimensional level changes.

The exercises provide a way of accessing bodily support for expressive movement in space and can be used to develop the dancer's and the actor's instrument. The goal is movement that comes from the core, is organized and supported for access to choices, and is potent and specific.

Body attitude

While most of the Laban and Bartenieff work is about the changing and accommodating people do in response to contextual and expressive needs, observers can note the basic "set" of a body in a particular attitude, or held shape. The categories Laban identified are Wall, Ball, Pin and Screw.

A wall-like body attitude is the wide-stanced, planted and somewhat flattened presentational mode of some people. The impression such folks give off is that of a wall—impenetrable and difficult to get beyond or around. The wall is also useful in confrontations, when a barrier needs to be set up between one person and another. In some cases, setting up the body as a wall is not useful.

A ball-like body attitude is often seen on those roly-poly body types who look like they could "roll with the punches"—literally. A pin-like body attitude is a narrowed up-and-down lengthening that gives the impression of a focused but possibly constricted perspective. A screw-like body attitude is a propensity for twisting towards or away from the object of the gaze.

Body Attitude is often the baseline for a character in a play or for a particular dance style. One can think of it as the launching point for growth or evolution, a point of departure.

Practice

Leading/Speaking from Body Parts: Practice experiencing moving and speaking from the heart, the head, the "gut", the pelvis, the feet, etc. and note what different characters and qualities emerge from each.

Try using different Body Attitudes for the same type of exploration.

Changing Organization: Practice movement that is organized by body half; i.e. right-side vs. left-side and upper half vs. lower half. How do you view the world differently from each organizational set? Does your perception change? Are new characters created? Then practice contralateral organization and see how perception and character shift.

Voice Work: Find the particular vocal origin in the body for different characters: for example, a duchess or duke, a clown, a scientist, a homeless person. Note how the voice is supported, or not supported by a variety of body-level organizations, counter-tensions, groundedness or body-level connections.

THE EFFORT LEVEL

Laban described four separate qualities of movement: flow, weight, space (or focus) and time. Each of these occurs along a continuum, and each reflects a change in attitude towards a particular factor.

Flow describes the ongoingness of movement and can be defined by the extremes of bound flow (capable of stopping at any moment) and free flow (continual releasing of the flow of movement).

Weight effort describes the attitude towards power and overcoming gravity and is defined by the extremes of strong weight effort (capable of pushing a piano across the floor or overcoming an obstacle) and light weight effort (rarified, buoyant surmounting of gravity).

Space effort can be single (direct) or multi-focused (indirect or flexible).

Time effort is a change in attitude towards time, as defined by the opposites of quickness or acceleration (a hastening of time) and sustainment (a lingering in time).

Efforts tend to occur, stylistically, in pairs (called States) and in threes (called Drives). States are read as moods; while Drives are fully loaded moments of full expressivity. Individuals and characters in plays tend to operate in States, and to reveal more about themselves in Drives.

Figure 4.4 Free flow

Figure 4.5 Bound flow

Figure 4.6 Strong weight

Figure 4.7 Light weight

Figure 4.8 Three examples of direct space effort

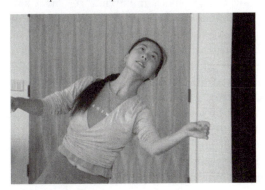

Figure 4.9 Indirect space effort

STATES

    Weight and Space = STABLE
    Time and Flow = MOBILE
    Weight and Time = RHYTHM
    Space and Flow = REMOTE
    Weight and Flow = DREAM
    Space and Time = AWAKE

DRIVES

    Weight, Space, Time = ACTION (no Flow and therefore no transitions or ongoingness from one moment to the next: the most externally and task-oriented Drive)

Space, Weight, Flow = SPELL (no Time and therefore a kind of spell is cast)

Weight, Flow, Time = PASSION (no Space and therefore no attention or investigation of the moment: the most internally-oriented Drive)

Space, Time, Flow = VISION (no Weight and Space, Time, Flow = VISION (no Weight and therefore no sense of personal power or intention within the moment)

Practice

Building personal style: Try activities such as making breakfast by primarily using a single effort in extreme; i.e. direct space or focus effort, or free flow, or strong weight, etc. Practice each one and note what tasks are easier with each effort factor. In this way, one can build a repertoire of expressive components.

Adding to the palette: After exploring each effort quality, decide which of them one is least likely to use expressively. Explore the full range of that factor and write a journal about the experience. Try using the factor in a variety of circumstances: while taking a walk, while in conversation, in a store, taking a shower, etc.

Using effort in improvisation: Create a dyadic situation in which a task is shared with another mover and enter into the improvisation using one of the eight effort qualities. Note how each mover adapts and changes qualities in order to communicate and complete the task.

THE SPACE LEVEL

Laban's work differs from many other somatics or body-based systems of movement because of his rich understanding of space, not as a separate and simply quantifiable entity but as a part of the interaction of inner and outer phenomena. In fact his original model for the analysis of movement consisted of Body (the action and inner world), Effort (the mediator of inner and outer through expression) and Space (the environment in which movement occurs).

He was, as we have seen in Part I, fascinated by both the geometric and the mystical aspects of spatial analysis. His space harmony work, including several "scales," draws on the artist/researcher's multi-focused understanding of the beauty, the drama and the mathematical calculations that unpack our relationship to the world around us.

If we think of personal and general space as our own real estate, it is easier to understand that each of us is drawn to particular aspects or places within that real estate. Some people are expansive in their use of space; some are specific and occupy well-defined segments of the full range of possibilities.

Space is alive in the sense that each mover infuses particular aspects of space with his/her energy. Some may limit the direction of that energy in space, honing it to a single dimension or plane; others "light up the room." Space is the container for effort and shape, and the architecture for actions.

One-dimensional space

The dimensions are defined as single spatial pulls with two polar ends. The Vertical Dimension is an Up-Down pull and relates directly to gravity. The Vertical Dimension divides the body into horizontal halves and therefore elucidates the side-side Horizontal Dimension, an imaginary spatial pull that bisects the body into upper and lower halves.

Put these two lines together and what is revealed is the Sagittal Dimension, a line that is pulled to the front and back of the body, completing the cross of axes. Laban devised a movement scale that follows these spatial pulls, called the Dimensional, or Defense Scale.

Figure 4.10 The three dimensions

The dimensional scale requires that the mover inhabit each dimension fully and with counter-tension: the vertical dimension is the first phrase, the horizontal dimension the second phrase and the sagittal dimension the third phrase. A mover may go from PLACE HIGH to PLACE LOW, and then cross over the midline in the horizontal dimension to PLACE ACROSS and PLACE OPEN, then to PLACE BACK and PLACE FRONT. The order of the sequence matters less than the dynamic tension between points or placements in space. When one reaches for PLACE HIGH, for example, one feels the counter-pull to PLACE LOW and then the pulls are reversed; with the PLACE LOW reach becoming the primary movement and the PLACE HIGH pull as the counter-tension.

Two-dimensional space—planes

The spatial pulls combine to produce planes in space. Planal movement is common in western cultures, and each plane is affined with particular ways of operating or presenting the self.

The combination of the horizontal and vertical dimensions result in what is called the vertical, or door plane. This plane is often seen in "ta-DAH!" moments, and is also known as the plane of presentation.

The combination of the horizontal and the sagittal dimensions result in the horizontal, or table plane. This plane is where spinning and twisting, skating, gathering and scattering tend to take place. It is also known as the plane of communication.

The third plane is the combination of the vertical and the sagittal dimensions and is called the sagittal, or wheel plane. Somersaults and other gymnastic activities take place in the wheel plane, as do bicycling and many other sports activities. It is also called the plane of operations.

Performers can use the selection of possible orientations to the space to create characters or diversity of pattern. Leaders can learn to "read" the preferences of clients and team members, and attune to, oppose, or balance out those people.

Three-dimensional movement—the cube

Combinations of three dimensions, or spatial pulls, become diagonals; extremes of far reach space that crisscross the body's center from one corner of an imaginary cube to the opposite corner. Laban devised the Diagonal Scale to explore these extremes of personal space. The Diagonal

Figure 4.11 The three planes

Scale is a great way to warm up and energize the performer and the stage space, and is often used by actors, with the accompanying effort drive configurations, to practice a full range of active energies.

There are eight corners of the cube that are connected via four diagonals:

FRONT-RIGHT-HIGH to BACK-LEFT-LOW
FRONT-LEFT-HIGH to BACK-RIGHT-LOW
BACK-LEFT-HIGH to FRONT-RIGHT-LOW
BACK-RIGHT-HIGH to FRONT-LEFT-LOW

When performing the diagonal scale, the above sequence is initiated entirely from one side/one arm of the body. When the other side/

Figure 4.12 Two of the diagonals within the cube

arm of the body initiates, the sequence is the same, but the right-left directions are reversed. In this way, the mover has to adapt the torso and pelvis in crossing the midlines of the body, creating deeper and more complex involvement of the body with the space. The most difficult point or tension to head towards, when leading with the right arm, for example, is often the BACK-LEFT-HIGH corner of the cube. In order to fully experience the three-dimensionality, the pelvis remains facing forward, and the arm/shoulder/torso shapes and accommodates with the fullest possible counter-tension and deep rotation in the joints.

The more dimensions of space are being accessed, the deeper in the joints the movement needs to reach, and the more complex the body-space connection is. When any movement into space feels tense or too difficult, it is almost always possible to deepen flexion in the joints, release into more rotation in the joints, and reach further into the space. The deepening has to happen in the joints that are proximal to the body part(s) initiating into space, but also in the opposing prox-imal joints, in order for the counter-tension to allow the mover to reach further into space from a deeper part of the body.

The corners of the cube are best found by feeling the three dimensional pulls equally. If one dimension or another takes over, the tension and counter-tension will not be fully felt, the movement will become two-dimensional. In this way, it can lose its potency and clarity, as well as expressivity.

Practice

In addition to simply practicing the diagonal scale, try telling a story about a scary event, or rehearsing a monologue that describes action after doing the diagonal scale fully on both sides. Notice the vocal changes, the gestural differences and the ability of the torso to support the meaning and the expression of the story.

On beyond three dimensions—transverse movement

Transverse movement is full of ever-changing spatial pulls that move between the clear lines described above. The mover changes form and is pulled off-vertical in constant change. The following series of pho-tographs may give a sense of how rich such movement can be:

Figure 4.13 Imagine the above photos in sequence and transverse movement can be seen

Laban devised many scales in order to encourage his students to explore transverse movement, including the Axis Scale, the A-Scale and the B-Scale. Each of these scales follows movement that transverses within the icosahedron (a sphere-like, twenty-sided crystalline form), shifting dimensions and planes with each phase. As the movement unfolds, each spatial pull both calls the mover to it and the mover is called to the next point, resulting in the ever-changing adapting described above and demonstrated in the photos.

Laban saw space as a dynamic and ever-changing canvas, not as points to hang movement on. "The essential contrasts of space directions felt by everybody are not so much the static-dimensional ones than the more mobile icosahedral-surface diagonals," he wrote (NRCD notes).

The symbols that Laban and others derived for those points in space were never meant to be static destinations for movement, but rather, a map for possibilities, energies and change. "Connections with or deviations from non-contrasting corners (of the planes) give rise to bends and twists, especially if it is compressed," he wrote of transverse movement (NRCD notes).

The bending and twisting he described are used today as warm-ups for dancers and actors, and as ways to open up the body into the realm of possibilities. We are not stuck with the access to space we have developed out of habit and preferences; we can expand and open up new vistas.

Practice

Explore characters that emerge from one-dimensional and two-dimensional (planal) movement. For example, what kind of movement and communicative possibilities are created when the mover limits him/herself to the vertical dimension only? The horizontal? The sagittal?

What kind of personality uses the door, table and wheel planes, respectively? And what characters can be developed based on transverse movement?

Another suggestion: try speaking and moving text in one aspect of space only:

"O that this too, too solid flesh would melt" is a different statement when it is spoken from the vertical dimension than it is when it is spoken from the sagittal dimension. Try all the dimensions.

Explore well-known characters with different planes or diagonals. Examples: Blanche du Bois, Prospero, Didi and Gogo, Tartuffe, Auntie Mame, Macbeth, etc. Where does each character seem to operate from?

Try improvisational scenes with characters operating from different planes. Example: two roommates trying to make breakfast separately in a small kitchen; with one tending to be in the horizontal plane and the other in the sagittal plane.

The Cocktail Party: Characters enter the party in various spatial forms: dimensions, planes, diagonals, transverse or icosahedral movement. As the improvisation unfolds, who each character is can be discovered, a name and occupation derived. Vocal patterns emerge, informed by the space and effort aspects of the character.

The scales are described and notated in Cecily Dell's *A Primer for Movement Description* but it is difficult to follow these without knowing the notation symbols. Ideally, one learns the scales from a Certified Movement Analyst, but it is also possible to simply explore one-dimensional, two-dimensional (planes), three dimensional and transverse movement in a more general sense through activities such as sports, folk and world dance forms, and martial arts.

THE SHAPE LEVEL

Shape is a recently identified category and, like the rest of Laban Movement Analysis, addresses the changing human form, in both shape and attitude. Shape is about the how the body changes shape in relationship to others. "Others" can be other movers, the space itself, or objects. There are three "modes" of shape change, or three different levels of relationship that human beings engage in.

Shape-flow

Shape-flow supports the body changing its form only in relationship to itself. People in shape-flow are growing and shrinking, twisting, breathing, self-referencing and experiencing a relationship of self to self. There is no relationship to others, to space or to any external event or object. Shape-flow appears when people are daydreaming, grieving, just going through the motions, taking care of themselves or are simply self-involved.

Imagine the way an infant changes shape as he/she is picked up by the mother, or the rocking back and forth of someone in deep grieving. Notice the self-involved dancer on the dance floor or the dreamy look on a young lover's face. All of these people are likely to be changing shape in relationship only to themselves and will be unaware of people around them. This is shape-flow.

Directional shape

Spoke-like and arc-like movement that bridges from self to the environment or an object or person is the second tier of shape. Directional movement is often that of the professional handshake, giving directions, the traffic cop, the cheerleader—anyone who is connecting self to space for expressive or utilitarian purposes.

Picture two business men talking and describing their latest deal, or punching each other in the shoulder. Notice the clear pathways, directions and intentional movement of someone doing American Sign Language. Recall the "ta-DAH!" throwing of the arms up in the air of a magician after finishing a trick. Directional movement can be arc-like, describing a boundary around the body, or spoke-like, penetrating the space between and bridging to an object.

Shaping

Shaping denotes a rich interaction between self and other; a constantly changing and responsive relationship that is mutual and sophisticated. One can think of it as molding or carving through and with space or a person. Hugs are examples of shaping, as is the urban hip-hop multiphased handshake that young men do with each other.

Practice

Practice shape-flow through meditative practices, rocking, fitness practices or any activity that allows one to move in relationship to oneself without the necessity of attending to the outer world.

Directional movement needs little practice. Most of our formalized human interactions naturally occur using directional movement (think about the business handshake). Observe traffic cops and business lunches to clarify what directional movement looks like.

Shaping is supported by full-bodied interactions, and one of the best ways to access it (aside from lots of good hugs) is through contact improvisation. Improvisation in which the body molds and adapts to other bodies, or to the floor, objects, or simply the space can be a great way to practice shaping.

Other Exercises: Try shaking hands in each mode to clarify the level of interaction or relationship.

Figure 4.14 Dancers shaping around each other and with the space

Thirty-second encounters: two actors enter the space from opposite sides and encounter each other. Without speaking, they size each other up, while maintaining shape-flow, directional or shaping mode. As they interact further, they either stay in the same mode or shift modes in relationship to the other. They separate and go to the opposite side from where they began. Unpack the encounter and describe what happened between the two characters.

Open scenes: Three scenes can be prepared; one that is about two people Meeting, one about two people waiting for something to happen (Maintaining), and one about two people separating (Leaving). The Meeting scene can be done with both people in shape-flow, one in shape-flow and one using directional movement, one in shape-flow and the other in shaping, or any other combination. The same choices can be applied to the Maintaining scene and the Leaving scene. Notice how the meaning changes with different combinations and how modes of shape change can clarify relationships.

AFFINITIES

Body, effort, shape and space are aspects of movement but they are not discrete features. How they occur together and under what circumstances particular combinations tend to appear comprise personal style and behavior. Each individual has distinct features, but there are also tendencies and patterns that signify belonging to a particular cultural group or geographic home. Many people adapt behaviors according to the context in which they are in; for example, work behaviors and style are not necessarily the same as relaxation behaviors or style.

But as revealing as such patterns are, Laban also identified shared preferences; particular combinations of shape and effort, or effort and space, or shape and space that tend to occur more universally, just because human beings have the bodies we have, and the same forces act on the body, such as gravity.

He called these shared preferences affinities. It is important to understand that Laban was not saying, nor are present-day movement analysts promoting the idea that there is anything correct or right about these affinities. Just because we tend to see a specific combination does not mean that they are more or less functional or expressive than other possible combinations. In fact, highly dramatic moments are often characterized by counter-affinities; combinations that are the opposite of what an observer expected to see.

Effort and space affinities

The vertical dimension is affined with weight effort. Both verticality and weight effort deal with a relationship to gravity, particularly in overcoming the pull of gravity in different ways. When one is moving toward Place High, or the upper end of the vertical dimension, one tends to use an increasing light weight effort, or a delicate levity. When one is moving toward Place Low, or the lower end of the vertical dimension, one tends to use an increasing strong weight effort, or compacted power. The horizontal dimension is affined with space effort, or focus. The horizon is something people often scan, after all. When one is moving away from the midline while opening in the side-side spatial pull, one tends to use indirect space effort or a multi-focused attitude, as one might open wide to take in the horizon, taking much in at once. When one is moving across the body or midline, a single focus, or direct space effort is used. The example Laban often gave is threading a needle: a task that requires a narrowing of the gaze, and one that is supported when one threads towards the opposite side of the body from the hand that is being used for the task.

The sagittal dimension is affined with time effort. People think of moving forwards and backwards in time, although time effort is an attitude, not a calculation. In Laban's time, the affinity for moving into the back space with quick time effort, as when jumping back from touching a hot stove, would be a common response. The affinity of moving forward in space with sustained time effort, decelerating as if to sneak up on somebody, also makes sense. But in Laban's time, the kind of fast cars and speed addictions we now have were not so prevalent. And so, observers often note the shift in affinities in the sagittal from moving forward in sustainment to moving forward with quickness. This is, after all, how cars work. People also tend to back up cars with sustainment rather than quickness, thereby practicing the counter-affinity, and replacing the affinity with its opposite.

Practice

Try the dimensional scale with the affinities:

UP with light
DOWN with strong
RIGHT OPEN with indirect
RIGHT ACROSS with direct
BACK with quick
FRONT with sustained

Then try the scale with the COUNTER-affinities. Note the dramatic effects of each, with the possible exception of the sagittal dimension. The counter affinity may not be so dramatic there, since so many people find the affinity strange and the counter-affinity familiar.

UP with strong
DOWN with light
RIGHT OPEN with direct
RIGHT ACROSS with indirect
BACK with sustained
FRONT with quick

The planes also have affinities and counter-affinities. Each plane, with two dimensions combined will have an affined STATE, or combination of two effort factors. It is important to note that flow effort is not affined with any dimensions in space, since flow flows where it wants to flow!

The vertical plane, consisting of both a vertical as well as a secondary horizontal pull, is affined with both weight and space effort, which in combination yields the STABLE state. If flow is added, the drive that is affined with the vertical (or DOOR) plane is the Spell Drive. If one thinks of a magician, or a sorceress casting a spell, the vertical plane (also called the plane of presentation) is often used.

The horizontal plane, consisting of both a horizontal as well as a secondary sagittal pull, is affined with both space and time effort, which in combination yields the AWAKE state. If flow is added, the drive that is affined with the horizontal (or TABLE) plane is the Vision Drive. If one thinks of someone gazing at the horizon and thinking about a lot of things, the horizontal plane is often used.

The sagittal plane, consisting of both a sagittal as well as a secondary vertical pull, is affined with both time and weight effort, which in combination yields the RHYTHM state. If flow is added, the drive that is affined with the sagittal (or WHEEL) plane is the Passion Drive. If one thinks of a passionate dance, where the dancer is throwing him or herself around without paying attention to where he/she is going, the sagittal plane (also called the plane of operation) is often used.

The diagonal scale and action drive

The diagonal scale consists of four diagonals that cross all of the body's midlines, going from the corner of an imaginary cube to the exact opposite corner. The affinities therefore are as follows:

> FRONT-RIGHT-HIGH = FLOAT (Sustained, Indirect, Light)
> to
> BACK-LEFT-LOW = PUNCH (Quick, Direct, Strong)
> to
> FRONT-LEFT-HIGH = GLIDE (Sustained, Direct, Light)
> to
> BACK, RIGHT, LOW = SLASH (Quick, Indirect, Strong)
> to
> BACK, LEFT, HIGH = DAB (Quick, Direct, Light)
> to

FRONT, RIGHT, LOW = WRING (Sustained, Indirect, Strong)
to
BACK, RIGHT, HIGH = FLICK (Quick, Indirect, Light)
to
FRONT, LEFT, LOW = PRESS (Sustained, Direct, Strong)

These affinities are not what is always seen, nor are they goals or destinations. Characters in plays can play an action, but the action is always in service of a goal or need. Laban's work has often been reduced to the above eight Action Drives, within the Diagonal Scale, thereby leading many to believe that a character's personality can be defined within one of the eight action drives. For example, an actor might base an entire character on the Effort Action Drive of DAB, as in, "she was a DAB." Characters, however, grow and change within a play, often based on new circumstances, interactions, and encounters, just as people do in "real life." Effort MODIFIES action, as opposed to BEING action. A DAB is not a personality characteristic so much as it a way of doing an action. So even though the drive configuration is called Action Drive, it is how an action is performed, and not the action itself.

Effort and shape affinities

Shape can be a container for effort in that, as the shape changes, the context changes and the effort shifts as well. For example, when the mover is performing a spoke-like directional movement across the body, direct space effort may be used. When the mover shifts into an arc-like movement that opens up, indirect space effort may be used.

Shape-flow, while not affined with space or with space-effort, often reveals some precursors or shadow efforts, such as a propensity for evenness, abruptness, fluctuations, low intensity or high intensity.

Directional movement does connect into space and can be highly effortful. An upwards movement might be informed by light weight effort; a downwards movement by strong weight effort. The above examples of sidewards across movement leading to direct space effort and side-wards open movements yielding indirect space effort are also common. Directional movement forwards might be sustained and tentative, and a hand thrust backwards with quickness might also be seen.

Shaping may include affined efforts or counter-affinities. As stated above, highly dramatic moments may engender opposing effort, shape and space statements. Carving through the space with arms and torso using strong bound effort is the hallmark of a certain style in contemporary dance, as is a widening/spreading with direct space effort or advancing with quickness and retreating with sustainment.

Practice

Explore well-known scenes, such as the witches' scenes in *Macbeth*, *Who's Afraid of Virginia Woolf?*, *The Glass Menagerie*, *Tartuffe*, etc. using affinities and counter-affinities. Decide which work best for the scenes and characters.

Create a phrase of movement and try it with the affinities and the counter-affinities. Decide which is preferable for the purpose and style of the movement.

OTHER CONCEPTS

Effort "Load"

How many qualities are combined in a particular expressive moment? The more effort configurations that are in drives, the more "loaded" we say someone is expressively.

Phrasing

Movement components are organized in phrases, or meaningful units of patterns and combinations. Phrasing can be even and uninteresting, or spicy and unexpectedly expressive. Some people use a lot of swing phrasing, a rise and fall of combinations. Some have long ongoing phrasing, difficult to interrupt, and some have short clipped phrases or phrases that trail off into nothingness. Some folks are explosive or impulsive, with lots of energy at the beginning of the phrase, and some are impactive or emphatic, saving the intensity for the end of the phrase. In cohesive groups and relationships, it is easy to observe how people adjust their natural phrasing patterns to attune or cohere, leading to moments of empathy and synchrony. It is also easy to see when people are not able to adjust their phrasing to attune or adapt, keeping them out of the club, so to speak.

Definition of a phrase: A phrase is an organization of the expression into meaningful segments that have a beginning, a middle and an end.

Phrases can have punctuation as well, such as a period, exclamation, or a dot, dot, dot … sense. Phrasing is usually connected up to breathing patterns, and often last as long as a breath lasts. Phrases can be very long and ongoing, short and clipped or of mixed length.

Types of phrasing

- Even: unchanging monotones
- Swing: Regular up and down organization of expressivity, as a swing
- Explosive/Impulsive: Phrases that are "loaded" expressively in the beginning segment of the phrase
- Emphatic/Impactive: Phrases that are "loaded" expressively at the end of the phrase
- Crescendo: Phrases that build to a more loaded ending
- Decrescendo: Phrases that diminish expressively as they unfold

Practice

Watch talk show interviews and note the adjustments the host makes to the phrasing of different guests. See if one can note what kinds of phrasing preferences, body part usage, tensions, organizations, effort, spatial patterns, or shape modes the guest uses, and how the host adapts to those.

Listen to someone telling a story and practice drawing a line as they speak, pausing when they pause, responding with the line as the story gets more or less expressive (or "loaded"). Then graph their gesture life as they tell the same story again. Compare phrasing length and types between vocal patterns and gesture patterns.

LABAN'S LEGACY

Only a few of the people who studied directly with Rudolf Laban are still alive, but all of them speak about his legacy in similar terms.

Geraldine Stephenson, the British theatrical choreographer (the British mini-series, *The Six Wives of Henry the Eighth* and countless West End musicals), said that nowadays dancers and actors tend to merely do what they feel, rather than attacking the objective. "Too much is left to the students," she said. There is value in defining and clarifying the action needed to get across a particular idea. Laban's work is valuable, she went on to say, because movement is meaningful, not simply attractive. Characters have conflicts and internal struggles and these are manifested onstage in movement.

Even in ballet, objectives need clarification and specific qualities can reveal not only the character and storyline, but can further specify and differentiate abstract moments as well. The late Kurt Jooss said:

> Back in the 1920s we used to say you can say anything in dance. This was grossly overestimated. We have learned in the meantime that not everything is a good subject for dance. I think dance is an art of the will, of acting, of doing. Music is sentiment and feeling. Dance is AFTER the feeling. Then the will will develop a movement, the action. In action we will find dance.
>
> (Partsch-Bergsohn and Jooss, 2002)

Sam and Susi Thornton spoke about Laban's leadership and charisma as well: "It's flow which demarks the great from the merely good," Sam said (Interview, June 30, 2004). Flow is what carries us through shifting relationships of one moment to the next.

Warren Lamb, Laban's student and a well-known management consultant, has said that Laban's movement profile revealed his visionary approach and his virtuosity as the basis for his charisma. The particular combination of elements that Laban used defined him as a generous man who illuminated every encounter he had.

What does Laban have to offer performers and choreographers in the twenty-first century? Antja Kennedy, a dancer/choreographer in Bremen, Germany feels that he developed a range of possibilities and the idea that there is much more than what one usually thinks of. Choreographers can look beyond their own preferences.

When Antja was a dancer working with many different choreographers, communication and interpretation were often difficult. When she worked with a Laban-trained person, however, there was a common language with which to clarify the intention. Communication went faster and was much easier. She could recall the phrase and self-observe, remembering what she had done. Antja pointed out that to be a good performer, one must integrate space and effort. One of her colleagues told her that she had much clearer expressive space after her Laban training. But what Antja valued most was the integration of all the components of movement into what is called a dynamosphere: a space full of potential and expressivity, interaction and clarity. Full expression is greater than the sum of the parts and provides for exponential possibilities.

The integration of body and space in current dance practice can be challenging. Some choreographers are OK with dancers working in pain, struggling to perform movement they do not understand. The dancers are not integrating the various parts into a coherent whole. It is fine, says Antja, to dance about disintegration, but a harmony has to precede discord in the dancer's body. The movement message may be about disintegration, but the dancer cannot fall apart while performing; he/she must begin with integration of all the parts and then let the disconnections happen.

When dancers watch a choreographer give them movement, they may not notice the emphasis on space or mode of shape or flow. Dancers just imitate the sequence and general shape of the movement, without addressing or absorbing the details of style, initiation of movement, effort or relationship. When to linger in time, when to release from the diaphragm, as opposed to releasing from the shoulders, where to focus, which body part is speaking the loudest at any time: such details are noticeable if only one knows how to look.

THE ARTIST/RESEARCHER

Laban's movement analysis transcends the boundaries between theory and practice. The traditional "page or the stage" split is no longer viable for many reasons, not the least of which is the current trend towards more thoughtful, socially and politically emancipatory performance work. The choreographer and the dancers both need a necessary understanding of theory and practice, as we can see from watching William Forsythe's explorations of twisted diagonals and flattened icosahedra; Pina Bausch's complexly expressive social commentary; Bill T. Jones' improvisation-based explorations of identity issues and Mark Morris' technically challenging movement patterns.

Kinesthetic intelligence, if not genius, is a requirement for the performer of today. Part of that intelligence is the ability to be specific and precise with execution and expression at the same time. A great deal of what is called "release technique," as well as popular somatics practices (Pilates, Alexander, Feldenkrais, etc.) has been informed by Bartenieff's fundamental exercises and principles, which in turn were based on Laban's demonstration that body actions impact space, and vice versa, that organization of expression affects functionality and vice versa, and that changing context changes how we move.

The dancer/performer of today needs to have choices and to be able to adjust and accommodate to extreme expectations. Even though the Laban/Bartenieff work is not a style or technique per se, the basic movement intelligence one develops through the work can clarify what is being asked, can provide a rich selection of possibilities for new vocabulary, and can provide underlying fundamental principles for execution of complex movement.

At the same time, today's performers must be able observers of both highly refined dance patterns and pedestrian movement. LMA is used to unpack movement patterns in many ways: cultural signifiers, personal style and effectiveness of nonverbal communication skills.

Cultural signifiers: As the world shrinks and cross-cultural amalgamations of dance and quotidian forms are developed, LMA practitioners can identify the baseline cultural markers or codes, and track the combined patterns. The goal of this process is to specify and authenticate movement so it is identifiable and accurate. In a world of diminishing boundaries and rampant appropriation, authenticity is an important value for both preservation and honest execution of movement.

Personal style: Every mover has a way of organizing expressive material so that it reflects inner attitudes. These combinations of Body, Effort, Shape, Space and Phrasing define character and style and can help to create the world of the piece or play. LMA is a type of map for tracking the choices made, as well as a way of suggesting possible new pathways or vocabulary. When one is trying to recreate a particular type of character or dance style, LMA can clarify the specifics of the original.

Effectiveness of nonverbal communication skills: More and more, LMA is used as a coaching tool for politicians, business leaders, actors, dancers and athletes, all of whom find themselves in the world of "performance." The first step of this approach to coaching is analysis of what the mover is already doing. LMA reveals how the mover is executing, adapting and coping with the environment already. In this sense, the analysis is a process of appreciating the details of the mover's inner and expressive life. Therefore, the first step in coaching is to value what is already there, both functionally and expressively.

From that inner life, options can be explored, and experiments with new material can happen. While an athlete may need to focus on honing in and shifting patterns slightly in order to be more specifically successful, a politician needs to add to his/her repertoire in order to listen to others more actively and accurately and to be able to respond, attune and advance the communication. The goal for the athlete is to refine the skills in order to increase accuracy, whereas the goal for the politician or business leader is to be more comfortable and authentic within his/her own skin. Both explorations are about further development of the movement vocabulary, but one is a more convergent process (the athlete) and the other more divergent.

For the artistic performer, the dancer and the actor, the process is both a refinement of specific skills and an expansion of vocabulary and options. The twenty-first-century performer must be both versatile and fully grounded in her/his personal style. He/she must be an accurate observer of the subtleties of character, personality and cultural style as well as a practitioner of a range of movement genres. The ability to analyze, reconstruct and replicate challenging or idiosyncratic movement is critical to portraying layered stories, subtle emotions, or virtuosic dance works.

Laban's original notion of bringing movement to everyone for the sheer joy of connecting with each other and expressing one's self fully has come full circle. Laban Movement Analysis brings everyone to the dance.

The process of researching/observing and creating/choreographing/performing is interactive and intrapsychic. In a sense, the mover is in constant dialogue with him/herself as well as with the world of relationships with others and the universe of possibility

Movement analysis builds a vocabulary and informs the ability of a mover to attune to others. From basic breathing patterns to shared body attitudes to adaptability in phrasing, effort, shape change modes and space, what was once a special talent for connecting with and understanding others who are different has become a possible access point for cross-cultural understanding and other ways of engaging across differences. Imagine the possibilities if diplomats were able to fully experience the inner attitudes of those with whom they were negotiating. Imagine the possibilities if world leaders could attune to each other and begin a process of making peace instead of war.

Constructing the world differently does not seem impossible when one sees options for adapting, sharing perspectives, trading outmoded and inefficient patterns for better and more viable behaviors.

From such rich layered understanding of the abilities of human beings to adapt and adjust, the promise of creativity and innovation emerges. The artist/researcher devises layered, honest, new work that frees us from standard beliefs or expectations. As Laban saw from his mountaintop in Ascona, and throughout his life, the horizon holds all the possibilities we need

FINAL THOUGHTS

From the day that Mary Wigman sought out Rudolf Laban on Monte Verita, theory and practice, analysis and innovation met, and created a dance of reason and joy, improvisation and craft, together.

From that time, we know that the movement moment is a propeller and a touchstone, dynamic and stabilizing. We have a choice to career about the world, unconscious and habituated, or to practice options, try out new patterns, experiment, innovate, choose, with consciousness and reflection. We can live our life as victims of time and space or as a work of art.

Evelyn Dörr (Interview, July 9, 2004) points out that "We have mapped DNA and we think we now know what 'life' is." It is not the analysis of movement that makes the dance happen; it is the access and range that dancers develop through the practice of discrete aspects of movement that, when combined with the soul and passion of the dancer or choreographer, create dance.

Laban understood how the individual spirit participates in and shapes community and constructs culture. No one really gets to be top banana in a true commune. Community is all about co-leadership and listening, not directing. But too often we believe we risk losing place and role and power when we start to participate in a communal effort. For people trying to create their own lives, building a community can be a struggle or an experiment. Actually, it is probably both, and the question becomes: who can practice differently enough to risk changing?

Laban's experiences at Ascona and Dartington show us that life is a construction. Through the "Yes, and ... " approach to improvisation that is still a part of our work, people have options and are empowered to create. Life and art are manifested through a process of conscious choices and happy accidents.

Movement itself allows people to reconnect to what they produce: dance as well as vegetables. Dance is something we create that can never be taken away. From the speech that Laban gave in Berlin in

1936, we can understand how dance, in the end, reveals the true nature of our aspirations, which includes the desire for an individual voice within a larger healthy community. From his work with movement choirs and the Vienna Festival in 1929, we can remember that through analysis and synthesis, through science and art, we can become masters of our crafts, and we can fall in love with our work again.

Movement is behavior, is communication. Movement reveals who we are and how we are. Because of Laban's contributions, performers, therapists, educators, athletes, community leaders, anthropologists, coaches, somatics practitioners, choreographers and directors have a tool with which to observe and adapt, to research and practice, to understand and to interpret, and to create and define.

The body speaks: we can know ourselves; we can sense changes and we can grow. Effort reveals: we can communicate with each other; listen, adapt, attune, express clearly. Space is palpable: we can occupy, define, and we can find patterns in complexity. Shape brings us into relationships: we can take care of ourselves, we can bridge to others and we can accommodate, sculpt, and share.

If we followed Laban's lead, we would honor the planet and ourselves more richly and more clearly. We would dance with the birds and the stars, yes, but more importantly, we would dance with each other. In a world of pain and strife, that would be miraculous.

BIBLIOGRAPHY

Bartenieff, Irmgard, with Dori Lewis (2002) *Body Movement: Coping with the Environment*. New York: Routledge.

Bartenieff, Irmgard Martha Davis and Forrestine Paulay (1970) *Four Adaptations of Effort Theory in Research and Teaching*. New York: Dance Notation Bureau.

Counsell, Colin (2004) "Dancing to Utopia: Modernity, Community, and the Movement Choir", Edinburgh: *Dance Research*, 22.2, Winter.

Davies, Eden (2006) *Beyond Dance. Laban's Legacy of Movement Analysis*. New York: Routledge.

Dörr, Evelyn (2003) "Rudolf von Laban: The 'Founding Father' of Expressionist Dance", in *Dance Chronicle*, Vol. 26, No. 1, pp. 1–29.

—— (2004) "Transformation of the Archaic: A Study of the Development and Stylistic History of Modern Dance, 1890–1938", unpublished paper.

Gleisner, Martin (1970) "Movement Choirs" in the *Laban Art of Movement Guild Magazine*, Nov., p. 10.

Green, Martin. (1986) *The Mountain of Truth: The Counter-Culture Begins, Ascona 1900–1920*. Hanover and London: New England Press.

Hodgson, John. (2001) *Mastering Movement: The Life and Work of Rudolf Laban*. New York: Routledge.

Laban, Rudolf (1920, translation date unknown) *Die Welt des Tanzers*. Partially translated by Richard Schröder, in the John Hodgson Collection, University of Leeds, UK.

—— (1924) "Das Tanztheater", in *Licht luft Leben Verlag Die Schonheit*, Dresden, Vol. XXII, translated by Sabine Fichter.

—— (1926) "Anatomie" in *Licht luft Leben Verlag Die Schonheit*. Journal published in Leipzig, Giesecke. Verlag Die Schonheit, Dresden and Leipzig, Vol. XXII, No. 1 p. 94, translated by Sabine Fichter.

—— (1926) *Choreographie*. Jena: Diederichs (out of print).

—— (1928) "Basic Principles of Movement Notation". *Schrifftanz*, Vol. I, No. 1, July, p. 32.

—— (1929). "The Renewal of the Movement in Theater" in *Singchor und Tanz*, Mannheim, 15 January, 1929, Vol. II, p. 561, translated by Sabine Fichter.

—— (1939) "Extract from an address held by Mr Laban on a meeting for community-dance in 1936". Translated by Laban March 10, 1939. Used with acknowledgment to the Dartington Hall Trust Archive, T/AD/3/A/5.

—— (1966) *Choreutics*. London: MacDonald and Evans. (annotated and edited by Lisa Ullmann).

—— (1971) *The Mastery of Movement*. London: MacDonald and Evans.

—— (1975) *A Life for Dance*. Princeton, NJ: Princeton Books.

—— (date unknown) NRCD notes. Surrey: National Resource Centre for Dance, University of Surrey.

Laban, Rudolf and F. C. Lawrence. (1974) *Effort: Economy in Body Movement*. London: MacDonald and Evans, 2nd edition.

Maletic, Vera. (1987) *Body-Space-Expression: The Development of Rudolf Laban's Movement and Dance Concepts*. Berlin/New York/Amsterdam: Mouton de Gruyter.

Newlove, Jean and John Dalby (2004) *Laban for All*. NewYork: Routledge.

Partsch-Bergsohn, Isa and Harold Bergsohn (1973) *The Makers of Modern Dance in Germany: Rudolf Laban, Mary Wigman, Kurt Jooss.* Hightstown, NJ: Princeton Books.

Partsch-Bergsohn, I., and Jooss, K. (2002) *A Talk with Kurt Jooss and Isa Partsch-Bergsohn* [video recording]. New York: Distributed by Insight Media.

Preston-Dunlop, Valerie (1963) *A Handbook for Modern Educational Dance.* London: MacDonald and Evans.

—— (1998) *Rudolf Laban: An Extraordinary Life.* London: Dance Books.

Preston-Dunlop, Valerie, and Susanne Lahusen (1990) *Schrifftanz: A View of German Dance in the Weimar Republic.* London: Dance Books.

Robb, D. (2005) "Staging the savage God: The grotesque in performance", *Modern Drama 48*(4).

Ullmann, Lisa, ed. (1971) *Rudolf Laban Speaks about Movement and Dance.* Addlestone, Surrey: Laban Art of Movement Centre.

Wasserman, Jerry (2004) "Monstrous Clowns: American Grotesques on the Canadian Stage" *Canadian Theatre Review* 120, pp. 33–37.

Wigman, Mary (1966) *The Language of Dance.* Connecticut: Wesleyan University Press.

Wigman, Mary and Walter Sorell, (1973) *The Mary Wigman Book: Her Writings.* Connecticut: Wesleyan University Press.

INTERVIEWS

June 30, 2004, Sam and Susi Thornton, UK.
July 2, 2004, Geraldine Stephenson, London, UK.
July 3, 2004, Valerie Preston-Dunlop, Blackheath, London, UK.
July 8, 2004, Antja Kennedy, Bremen, Germany.
July 9, 2004, Evelyn Dörr, Leipzig, Germany.

INDEX

Related titles from Routledge

Bertolt Brecht
Routledge Performance Practitioners series
Meg Mumford

All books in the **Routledge Performance Practitioners** series are carefully designed to enable the reader to understand the work of a key practitioner. They provide the first step towards critical understanding and a springboard for further study for students on twentieth-century performance, contemporary theater and theater history courses.

Bertolt Brecht is amongst the world's most profound contributors to the theory and practice of theater. His methods of collective experimentation and his unique framing of the theatrical event as a forum for aesthetic and political change continue to have a significant impact on the work of performance practitioners, critics and teachers alike.

This is the first book to combine:

- an overview of the key periods in Brecht's life and work
- a clear explanation of his key theories, including the renowned ideas of Gestus and Verfremdung
- an account of his groundbreaking 1954 production of *The Caucasian Chalk Circle*
- an in-depth analysis of Brecht's practical exercises and rehearsal methods.

ISBN13: 978-0-415-37508-5 (hbk)
ISBN13: 978-0-415-37509-2 (pbk)
ISBN13: 978-0-203-88210-8 (ebk)

Available at all good bookshops
For ordering and further information please visit:
www.routledge.com

Related titles from Routledge

Robert Lepage
Routledge Performance Practitioners series
Aleksandar Saša Dundjerović

All books in the **Routledge Performance Practitioners** series are carefully designed to enable the reader to understand the work of a key practitioner. They provide the first step towards critical understanding and a springboard for further study for students on twentieth-century performance, contemporary theater and theater history courses.

Robert Lepage is one of Canada's most foremost playwrights and directors. His company, *Ex Machina*, has toured to international acclaim and he has leant his talents to areas as diverse as opera, concert tours, acting and installation art. His most celebrated work blends acute personal narratives with bold global themes.

This is the first book to combine:

- an overview of the key phases in Lepage's life and career
- an examination of the key questions pertinent to his work
- a discussion of *The Dragons Trilogy* as a paradigm of his working methods
- a variety of practical exercises designed to give an insight into Lepage's creative process.

ISBN13: 978-0-415-37519-1 (hbk)
ISBN13: 978-0-415-37520-7 (pbk)
ISBN13: 978-0-203-09897-4 (ebk)

Available at all good bookshops
For ordering and further information please visit:
www.routledge.com

Related titles from Routledge

Mary Wigman
Routledge Performance Practitioners series
Mary Anne Santos Newhall

All books in the **Routledge Performance Practitioners** series are carefully designed to enable the reader to understand the work of a key practitioner. They provide the first step towards critical understanding and a springboard for further study for students on twentieth-century performance, contemporary theater and theater history courses.

A dancer, teacher and choreographer, Mary Wigman was a leading innovator in expressionist dance. Her radical explorations of movement and dance theory are credited with expanding the scope of dance as a theatrical art in her native Germany and beyond.

This book combines for the first time:

- a full account of Wigman's life and work
- a detailed discussion of her aesthetic theories, including the use of space as an "invisible partner" and the transcendent nature of performance
- a commentary on her key works, including *Hexentantz* and *The Seven Dances of Life*
- an extensive collection of practical exercises designed to provide an understanding of Wigman's choreographic principles and her uniquely immersive approach to dance.

ISBN13: 978-0-415-37526-9 (hbk)
ISBN13: 978-0-415-37527-6 (pbk)
ISBN13: 978-0-203-09898-1 (ebk)